Let Them Be Themselves

ACKNOWLEDGMENTS

Thanks are due to the following for the use of copyrighted material listed below:

Curtis Brown, Ltd. for "Good Books, Good Times!" by Lee Bennett Hopkins. Copyright © 1985 by Lee Bennett Hopkins; "School Talk" by Lee Bennett Hopkins. Copyright © 1992 by Lee Bennett Hopkins. Used by permission of Curtis Brown, Ltd.

Harcourt Brace Jovanovich, Inc. for an excerpt from "Pencils" in *Smoke and Steel* by Carl Sandburg, copyright 1920 by Harcourt Brace Jovanovich, Inc., and renewed 1948 by Carl Sandburg. Reprinted by permission of Harcourt Brace Jovanovich, Inc.

HarperCollins Publishers for "After English Class" from *Hey World, Here I Am!* by Jean Little. Text Copyright © 1986 by Jean Little. Illustrations copyright © 1989 by Susan G. Truesdell. Reprinted by permission of HarperCollins Publishers.

Felice Holman for "Who Am I?" from *At the Top of My Voice and Other Poems* (Charles Scribner's Sons, 1970). Used by permission of the author.

Simon & Schuster, Inc. for the quotation on page 207 from *Joys and Sorrows* by Pablo Casals: His Own Story as told to Albert E. Kahn. Copyright © 1970 by Albert E. Kahn. Reprinted by permission of Simon & Schuster, Inc.

Charlotte Zolotow for "School Day" from *All That Sunlight* (Harper & Row, 1967). Used by permission of the author, who controls all rights.

Let Them Be Themselves

Typography by Al Cetta

1 2 3 4 5 6 7 8 9 10

Third Edition

Library of Congress Cataloging-in-Publication Data
Hopkins, Lee Bennett.
  Let them be themselves / Lee Bennett Hopkins.—3rd ed.
    p.   cm.
  ISBN 0-06-023852-6
  1. Socially handicapped children—Education—United States—
Handbooks, manuals, etc. 2. Teaching—Aids and devices—Handbooks,
manuals, etc. 3. Activity programs in education—United States—
Handbooks, manuals, etc. 4. Children—United States—Books and
reading—Handbooks, manuals, etc. I. Title.
LC4091.H67 1992   91-19119
371.96'7—dc20   CIP

LEE BENNETT HOPKINS

Let Them Be Themselves

THIRD EDITION

HarperCollins*Publishers*

To Misha Arenstein—
Round Three.
LBH

Contents

Preface

Words From a Fellow Educator

This totally revised third edition of *Let Them Be Themselves* was completed more than two decades after the first edition appeared in 1969. In the Foreword to the first edition, and to the second edition, published in 1974, I stated: "Teachers are part of the momentous revolution that is taking place in America. In all sections of our country old institutional forms are being challenged; college campuses, suburbs, cities, rural areas, and the most remote environs all contribute to the cacophony of voices demanding changes. Change is on every educator's lips—new mathematics, new social sciences, new reading techniques."

In the interim, most schools, after operating with loosely organized programs, embraced back-to-basics programs attempting to meet the needs of inner-city children as well as those living in affluent suburbs.

While it is true that all children need carefully structured programs to achieve success, the programs that relied almost entirely on this textbook-oriented approach did little for the children of the 1970's, 1980's, or early 1990's.

Today—once again—we hear the cries of change. *Change!* Try the *new* computer-based programs, try *new* hardware, software, initiate whole-language programs, try the phonics approach. Try reaching every child on his or her own level—individualize. Try! Experiment! Change!

Teachers as educators can no longer be content with the methods of yesterday; we cannot remain static. Education is not what it was fifteen or thirty years ago—or even what it was yesterday. Whether teachers, parents, or citizens like it or not, whether they are motivated or not, they must become part of our quickly changing society. They have to know about such happenings as the space race, the latest comic book or television hero, or the location of formerly obscure, developing nations halfway across the globe.

We must all deal with the AIDS crisis; the thousands of children for whom a home is a cardboard box, a welfare hotel, or a concrete slab underneath an overpass; homeless children who do not attend school on a regular basis; children of divorce; latchkey children who come home from school with no one to greet them; increased violence in our schools due to drugs; the demands of millions of our forgotten minorities who cry out for the resolutions of old injustices.

Some adults say: "Kids today have everything! They

have their own computers, television sets, VCRs, designer clothes, money." While it is true that some children have all this, the many who do not have "everything" eagerly demand to share in the affluence of America.

Young people today, both the disadvantaged and the advantaged, are beset by a host of problems inherited from yesterday's young people who have aged and become parents, leaders, and educators: problems in the suburbs, integration, demands for technical skills as a condition for future employment, and enticements from every angle that say: "Come real close, but don't touch! Look, look, look! See, see, see! No! No! No!"

Clearly teachers today face an enormously difficult job. Society relies upon us to train tomorrow's wage earners, citizens, and parents. Teachers in twentieth-century America have a difficult assignment, but they do their job and hope for the very best.

I wrote *Let Them Be Themselves* with today's classroom teacher in mind. This revised and expanded volume is a compilation of innovative activities and ideas that have been successfully tried and tested throughout the United States, Puerto Rico, and Canada. The volume is a *has-been-done* book rather than a *how-to-do* book.

Language arts teaching that applies to *all* children encompasses basic components to aid in communication—speaking, listening, reading, writing, and thinking—as a means through which *all* children can be themselves.

In the more than two decades since this volume's original publication, America has continued to search for answers in our complex world of education.

Today one hears of "new" approaches to producing employable graduates of public schools. Whole language, process writing, and computer literacy can be only as successful as the teachers who offer them. In many cases, the most successful educators are those who focus on their students' abilities and competencies, catering to the needs of the individual, rather than attempting to meet state or national guidelines. As long as all students are expected to accept a passive role in the learning process, I fear the failures of the past will be repeated in the future.

I sincerely hope that this text will continue to help teachers-to-be, assist young teachers, and give experienced teachers some new ideas while they work under the everyday pressures in our schools.

Lee Bennett Hopkins
Scarborough, New York
January 1992

PART ONE

Who Are They? Who Am I?

The Improvement of Self-Image

WHO AM I?
Felice Holman

The trees ask me,
And the sky,
And the sea asks me
    Who am I?

The grass asks me,
And the sand,
And the rocks ask me
    Who I am.

The wind tells me
At nightfall,
And the rain tells me
    Someone small.

    Someone small
    Someone small
    But a piece
        of
        it
        all.

Many labels are attached to children—socially disadvantaged, culturally disadvantaged, children at risk, underprivileged, educationally deprived, lower class, lower socioeconomic strata, the segregated, intellectually deprived, the bilingual child, the dialectal child, the learning disabled, the migrant, the reservation child, the homeless—and many reasons are cited as to *why* children are labeled as such and *how* they became that way. Many preventive and remedial programs are being carried out: Some are effective; some are not.

Who are the children that make up the classrooms in today's schools?

Where do they come from?

They are the black and Puerto Rican children in schools of the inner cities—Harlem in Manhattan, Watts in Los Angeles, the Hough area of Cleveland, Bedford-Stuyvesant in Brooklyn. They also include children in poverty areas in all our major cities—Detroit, New Haven, Hartford, Chicago, Newark, Washington, Baltimore, and Miami.

They are the children of the migrant workers who follow crops from place to place as a means of livelihood, traveling from the San Bernardino Valley in California to Long Island in New York. They are the children in the Appalachians and the Cumberlands, scattered throughout Kentucky, Virginia, and Tennessee, and they are the Native American children of Papagos, Arizona. They are children who enter the United States from the West Indies, Cuba, Puerto Rico, Haiti, the Dominican Republic, and from South America—Chile, Ecuador, Argentina, Colombia, and Venezuela.

They are the children living in wealthy suburbs—Beverly Hills, California; Scarsdale, New York; Grosse Pointe, Michigan—who come to school with a myriad of family problems—from alcoholic and drug-addicted parents to dysfunctional families.

They are the children who enter school with many strikes against them, including uprooted family and home lives, language barriers, and, often, a distorted view of themselves.

Children develop a picture of themselves based on interaction with family, peers, and environment. For many children this picture is often distorted by the absence of a mother or father figure and by society's apparent rejection of them. In addition, the limited number of job opportunities available to minority-group adults sharply restricts the adult roles the child is able to see and emulate.

Family problems, language handicaps, and a multitude of social ills can take years and years of patience and struggle to deal with, but the improvement of the self-image of all children cannot wait. Deliberate efforts must begin immediately to raise their sights, arouse aspirations that can alter contructively the courses of young lives.

The following comments by children were recorded from various parts of the country. These remarks illustrate some of the negative ideas and misconceptions these children have with regard to their place in society—to their heritage—to themselves.

Two men visited a fifth-grade classroom in Oklahoma; one was white, the other black. When they were introduced to the children, a girl called out to the black visitor: "You-all can't be black! There ain't no black people in Oklahoma!" The gentleman assured her that there were indeed black people in the state; however, the child could not accept his remark. After a moment or two of deep thought, she stated: "You had to be born in Harlem first, and then go out to Oklahoma. Black people are born in Harlem before they go away from it!"

****

A fourth-grade child talking to his teacher asked: "Were you born white?"

The teacher replied, "Yes!"

"I was born white, too," stated the child, "but I turned Puerto Rican when I was one year old 'cause I was so bad!"

****

Another fourth grader revealed: "I feel like a yo-yo. On weekends I live with my daddy, during the week I live with Mom. During the summer I stay at my Aunt Doris' house. I wish I had one place I really felt I lived in."

****

****

A third-grade migrant child stated: "People don't like us. That's why we have to move around a lot. People don't like pickers like me and my sister."

****

A second grader commented: "The difference between black and white people is the way they act. We're black because we're bad, huh?"

****

A Native American child in a first-grade classroom asks: "Teacher, who am I?"

****

This is just a small sampling of the types of comments and responses children utter by the thousands day after day in classrooms near and far. Obviously, the child who fears that "black" means "bad" and that "Spanish-speaking" indicates ignorance, or a child coping with different home environments, can envision only a limited future. The classroom teacher, through the devices of field trips, media, children's literature, and human resources can provide broader horizons for children who are locked into the narrow boundaries of their immediate neighborhoods. Acquainting children with past and contemporary figures of importance who are of their own particular race, creed, or national background, or with those who have succeeded despite societal and environmental restrictions, can go a long way toward providing a child with a positive self-image.

To undo much of the damage that has been done is a complex task. We teachers must try, however, for we cannot afford to allow children to grow up into adulthood with such negative feelings, anxieties, and falsities about themselves and their role in today's civilization. And we must not assume that building a positive self-concept is a concern only of the disadvantaged child. In today's mechanized world, a world filled with constant change, *all* children need the strength that a healthy self-concept can provide.

What can we teachers do?

How can we do it?

There are no pat answers. Experimentation, imagination, and determined effort can provide the means to help youth find their place in life. The techniques offered below have been used, and have proved to be effective, as aids in improving self-image and developing positive concepts of children's cultural and racial backgrounds.

Look in the Mirror

We sometimes take a lot for granted. Many adults are totally unaware that some children come from homes where the only mirror is in the bathroom. This mirror is usually on the medicine chest, far out of reach of the average child. Small wall mirrors or inexpensive full-length mirrors placed in classrooms and in corridors at a child's-eye level give children the opportunity to really see themselves during the day—a privilege not afforded to many.

A variety of oral and written language activities has been sparked by the use of a mirror in the classroom. One second-grade teacher in an Appalachian classroom in Kentucky uses a mirror to have children role-play various parts. A large box is filled with hats of all kinds—a police officer's hat, a fire fighter's helmet, a sailor's cap, an astronaut's helmet, an airline captain's hat, discarded hats that were worn by mommies and daddies—that have been collected through the years. The children don the hats and go to the mirror. With either the teacher or another student, a child takes on the role that the hat suggests, freely converses about duties and responsibilities, or just has a good time.

In another classroom setting where this concept was tried, the teacher had the children talk into a tape recorder, later writing out some of their comments. This served as the basis for an innovative bulletin-board display called "In Your Everyday Hat." Hats were fastened to a bulletin board with comments prepared by the children underneath each one, such as:

UNDER THE STUDENT NURSES'S CAP
I must go now and take all the babies' thermometers out of their mouths.

UNDER A FLOWERY BONNETT
This is my Easter bonnet. It took three years to make
and it cost one million dollars, and that's a lot for a hat!

Besides having a chance to role-play, speak, and
listen, the boys and girls had the opportunity to see
themselves in creative and imaginative roles.

At the Glenmont Elementary School in Glenmont,
New York, the third Friday of each January becomes
Hat Day, a project initiated by Peter Rawitsch, a first-
grade teacher at the school. On Hat Day everyone in
the school dons a hat to celebrate the wide variety of
hats worn around the world.

Besides writing hat stories and poems, children create original hats and engage in other educational hat-
related activities—from performing the Mexican hat
dance to marching in a hat parade.

Sharing books about hats can further such activities.
Try one or all of these on "for size":

Geringer, Laura. *A Three Hat Day*. Illustrated by Arnold Lobel. Harper, 1985.

A delightful story of R. R. Pottle, the Third, who loves
hats and who meets and marries Isabel, who is a hat
lover too!

Keats, Ezra Jack. *Jennie's Hat*. Harper, 1966.

A book that is a natural to spark creative writing,
drawing, and talking about things to do with a very
plain hat.

Morris, Ann. *Hats Hats Hats*. Illustrated by Ken Keyman. Lothrop, 1989.

A wide variety of hats is introduced, illustrated with striking full-color photographs, depicting many faces from many cultures.

Roy, Ron. *Whose Hat Is That?* Illustrated by Rosmarie Hausherr. Clarion, 1987.

The appearance and function of eighteen types of hats, including a top hat, football helmet, and chef's hat, are shown and discussed. The book is illustrated with black-and-white photographs.

Seuss, Dr. *The 500 Hats of Bartholomew Cubbins*. Vanguard, 1938; reissued, Random House.

What child could resist the ever-popular, ever-humorous tale of Bartholmew Cubbins?

Slobodkina, Esphyr. *Caps for Sale*. Harper, 1947.

A classic tale about a peddler who sells caps and a band of monkeys who take them from him when he falls asleep.

A fourth-grade teacher in Hartford, Connecticut, uses mirrors to correlate science projects with language arts skills. He uses an excellent book, *Look at Your Eyes* by Paul Showers, illustrated by True Kelley (Harper rev. ed. 1992) to motivate such projects. Children look into mirrors and begin to really discover their own eyes. They look at the color, the size, the shape, at their eyebrows, eyelashes, and eyelids. They begin to discuss, analyze, to think critically about something they had taken for granted. The children talk, write, draw, and perform simple experiments to learn more about themselves—to discover how different each person is, yet how human beings are all so much the same.

Look at Your Eyes is one of Let's Read-and-Find-Out Science Books (Harper), a series that provides many titles of basic scientific information presented in a way early readers can cope with. Some other titles include *Your Skin and Mine* by Paul Showers, illustrated by Kathleen Kuchera (revised edition 1991); *Straight Hair, Curly Hair* by Augusta Goldin, illustrated by Ed Emberley (1966); *My Five Senses* (revised edition, 1989), *My Hands* (1990), both written and illustrated by Aliki; and *Ears Are for Hearing* by Paul Showers, illustrated by Holly Keller (1990).

Children can also have a great deal of fun using full-length mirrors to create life-sized replicas of themselves. While one child lies down on kraft paper, another child can trace his or her body outline. When the outline is finished and cut out, children can fill them in with crayons, paints, or collage materials to re-create themselves. Pieces of scrap fabric can be added, and buttons, belts, or other realia can be glued or stapled onto the figures. These life-sized creations can adorn classroom walls or school halls, and later children can take them home.

Instead of literally "making themselves," older girls and boys can assemble magazine and newspaper photographs, slogans, advertisements, and other items that reflect their individual tastes, interests, and viewpoints. These items can be pasted on their cutout figures.

Me-mobiles can also be constructed using mirror techniques. Drawings of children's eyes, noses, lips, ears, or other parts of their bodies, such as hands and feet, can be made. Thread the cutouts with string, yarn, or heavy thread and hang them from coat-hanger wire or short pieces of doweling. The finished mobiles can be hung from classroom ceilings.

Picture This

Photographs can be used in a variety of ways. Whenever possible, photographs should be taken of individuals and groups both in and out of the classroom, catching children in the act of solving various problems or making contributions to the class. Pictures can be taken of children reading books, working on art projects, or doing work at the chalkboard. Group shots can be taken of teams who won the relay race or of the group who came in first in the spelling bee. The camera also plays an important role during field trips. Mounting the pictures in books, and occasionally displaying them, provide children with an image of how they look and act in different candid situations.

Other ideas involving the use of photography appear throughout this volume.

The Sharing Box

A cardboard box can become Our Sharing Box. Books, toys, games, and hobbies can be put into the box for others to share during their free time. The contributor (or teacher) labels each item by attaching a card with his or her name on it. Things shared can be the basis for an oral language activity. Before items are placed in the box, children describe them and/or tell why they brought them in to share. The classroom teacher can use the children's comments as a basis for writing experience charts. Each day a list of the children's contributions can be noted:

Mario put a *top* in the box today.
Dolores put a *book* in the box today.
Juan put a *pencil* in the box today.

Children are able to learn many new words as a result of this activity; it also underlines the fact that every child has *something* worth giving.

The Welcome Back System

Children who are frequently absent from school can well benefit from a Welcome Back System, which has been used in many schools very successfully. Each child in the class chooses a buddy. When one or the other is absent from school for a day or for a period of time, the buddy goes to visit, telephones the absentee to find out why he or she was out, or brings home study assignments or notices. If a child is out due to illness, the buddy reports to the teacher, and the class sends a get-well card or letter. When the absent child returns to school, the buddy helps the child to fit back into the regular daily routines of the classroom.

Creative Calendars

Children can do research to find famous birthdays and anniversaries, or dates of inventions, special holidays, or events. With this information, weekly or monthly calendars can be created.

"Puerto Rico: A Holiday Calendar" is one example of a project initiated in several East Harlem schools where a high percentage of the population is Spanish-speaking. Among the items included are:

> JANUARY 11: This is a school holiday because it is the birthday of Eugenio Maria de Hostos. Hostos was a famous poet, educator, and political leader. In the schools, the children study his biography and learn about him as a writer and a politician. Flowers are placed at his monument at the university, and speeches are made in his honor.

> APRIL 16: This school holiday is José de Diego Day. Diego was a famous poet and writer. Children learn about his life in school. Flowers are placed at his statue, and his poems are recited in the schools.

JUNE 24: San Juan Batista Day is an important day in San Juan because San Juan Batista is the patron saint of San Juan. Each town has its own patron saint. Some towns begin to celebrate the day dedicated to the saint as early as nine days before.

Special activities take place during this time. For example, one day may be devoted to games, songs, and dances or musical groups in the town plaza; another day may be devoted to boat races. Entertainers move from town to town during the year to help celebrate the seventy-seven patron saints of the towns of Puerto Rico.

Other titles of calendars might include "A Black History Calendar," "South American Holidays," "People of the Islands," or "Great Native Americans."

Autobiographies

A collection of autobiographies, one page written by each child, can be put into a scrapbook and bound, or they can be placed around the room. This technique has been beneficial for introducing the children to student teachers, substitute teachers, paraprofessionals, and the many visitors who come in and out of an elementary classroom during the school year. Children also get to know about one another, and they enjoy reading about themselves. A photograph of each child to accompany his or her autobiography is a worthwhile addition.

Self-reflective collages can also introduce children to

classmates. Students can cut out letters to spell their names and use pictures or memorabilia to reflect individual tastes and personalities.

With the help of an art teacher, students can create outline silhouettes of their faces and attach them to large pieces of oaktag or construction paper. They can then look through magazines and clip out bits and pieces of things that reflect them—their personalities, moods, what is on their minds—highlighting anything from autumn's colors to a football game—sharing their individual "mind portraits."

Who Is the Child of the Week?

Each week of the school year a child in every classroom can be selected as The Child of the Week. Names can be drawn from a box, or it can be decided that children will be selected alphabetically by last name. The child selected prepares a bulletin-board display to tell the class about specific interests in sports, television shows, hobbies, pets, or books. The child's address and a list of family members might also be posted. When possible, a member of The Child of the Week's family— either an adult or a brother or sister who attends the same school—should be invited to the class to see the display. Students can draw from many sources—writing exercises, drawings, or photographs.

This idea has been used as a motivating device for interest in classroom and school affairs. It also serves to build up the self-image of even the most insecure or unhappy child in the classroom.

Hall of Fame

A Hall of Fame has been used in two ways. First, several schools have utilized this project to raise the children's occupational sights by having alumni elected to their school's Hall of Fame. People chosen are those who have distinguished themselves in various fields and include sports and entertainment personalities, business and industry leaders, as well as people in various professions. One school Hall of Fame boasts of a fashion designer for a leading department store, a scenic designer for the theater, an author, and a popular singing group. Each time a new member is added, a special ceremony that involves both the school and the community is planned.

A good volume to turn to in initiating such a project is *People Who Make a Difference* by Brent Ashabranner (Dutton, 1989), a book about everyday heroes and heroines, illustrated with black-and-white photographs by Paul Conklin. Readers will meet Ron Cowart, a Vietnam veteran, now a police officer, who spends time helping Southeast Asian refugees in Dallas; Margaret Gallimore, a mother who runs a hospice for people with AIDS; Frank Trejo, a karate master whose program for young people with severe disabilities improves their motor skills and their self-images; and Brother Ronald Giannoni, a Capuchin friar who feeds the hungry and houses homeless people in Wilmington, Delaware. The book reflects some of the many who are doing things on a local level to make the world a better place to live in, showing that one person *can* make a difference in society.

Second, classroom Halls of Fame have been developed. The children do research about famous personalities who are candidates for induction into the Hall of Fame. Campaigning can be done by individuals or by groups of children. The class can vote by secret ballot for new members to be honored. This type of activity can be an interesting one for children to carry out, for *they* can decide on rules and regulations for the operation of the project. Among classroom Halls of Fame selected by children have been a Contemporary Black Hall of Fame, which included Martin Luther King, Jr., Bill Cosby, and Martha Collins; a Sports Hall of Fame, which featured Jill Trenary, Babe Ruth, Wilt Chamberlain, and Greg Louganis; and a Music Hall of Fame, which included Cher, Leonard Bernstein, and Michael Jackson.

One resource to tap is a compact volume, *Contemporary Heroes and Heroines*, edited by Ray B. Browne (Gale, 1990), a guide to over a hundred twentieth-century figures and their achievements. The volume presents biographical portraits arranged in alphabetical order from Hank Aaron to Jeana Yeager, chosen after nine hundred public and school librarians were surveyed to define heroic traits and figures in the latter half of the twentieth century. Each entry features a black-and-white photograph of the personality, quotations, biographical data, an essay on each one's life and accomplishments, and sources of books and periodicals to consult for further reading and reference.

Another resource, published by Knowledge Unlimited, Inc., is a series of colorful, informative, 17" × 22" posters. Two of the sets are "Hispanic Heritage" and "Great Black Americans."

The Hispanic set features ten leaders from past and present: Simón Bolívar, Pablo Casals, Cesar Chavez, Henry Cisneros, Roberto Clemente, Ponce de León, Gabriel García Márquez, Rita Moreno, Katherine Ortega, and Pablo Picasso.

"Great Black Americans" details the lives and accomplishments of Martin Luther King, Jr., Jackie Robinson, Jesse Owens, George Washington Carver, Booker T. Washington, Harriet Tubman, Langston Hughes, Louis Armstrong, Ralph Bunche, and Thurgood Marshall. Write to the company for a free catalog describing these sets and other teaching materials. (The addresses of companies and organizations cited in this book appear in the appendix, beginning page 209.)

You can also encourage students to look in school or public libraries for biographies of some of the people they wish to fete.

So It's Their Birthday

The most important days of any school year are the children's birthdays. No matter what age children reach, they want their days to be remembered and shared with others. The following activities can be adapted for the various grades and can give a new look to the old custom of birthday celebrations.

Birthday Charts

In a Washington, D.C., classroom, early in the school year, each child tape-records his or her name and birth-date. This information is transcribed and placed on oaktag charts showing the days from September through August. When the special days arrive, activities are planned to make specific children feel proud of *their* days. Some children select a favorite poem to read; others relate something of interest, perhaps about where they were born, early childhood memories, or a hobby. Other children become messengers for the day or choose the game they enjoy most to play during the physical education period or recess. Class members make original greeting cards, presenting them to the birthday children at the close of the school day so they can take them home to share with family members.

The oaktag charts can take on a variety of themes and can be placed around the room for permanent display.

Twelve railroad cars cut from colored oaktag and labeled for each month can be connected on, above, or under a bulletin board to form Our Birthday Express. A small photograph of each child can be placed on the proper railroad-car. The same idea can be used to tie in with classroom interests. Rocket ships can lead to A Birthday Planet; stars can become A Sky of Birthdays; flowers can produce A Garden of Birthdays.

This Is Your Life

Committees might plan a booklet about each child's life. Discussions about what is involved in the creation of a biography can be held. Each committee can then set out to explore and investigate highlights of the child's life. They might write letters to parents, interview friends and relatives, or gather information from former teachers. With the collected data, and perhaps interesting photographs, they can prepare an attractive booklet to present to the birthday child.

Birthday Box

Several art or writing sessions might be planned to allow children to produce gift articles for a Birthday Box. When a birthday arrives, a gift is selected from the box while the class sings "Happy Birthday." A discussion can be held about who wrote or made the gift and why. Through this activity young children often have the opportunity to feel proud—whether they are giving the gift or receiving it.

Birthday Books

If possible, it is desirable to have on hand one or several volumes of stories and poems about birthdays to share with the class. Below is a selected list of some current and popular books for boys and girls:

Duncan, Lois. *The Birthday Moon.* Illustrated by Susan Davis. Viking, 1989.

"On your very next birthday/I'll give you a moon/On the end of a string/Like a golden balloon . . ." begins this fantasy illustrated in full color, about the wonderful things a child might do with the perfect birthday gift— the moon.

Gibbons, Gail. *Happy Birthday!* Holiday House, 1986.

In bright, full-color pictures and simple vocabulary, the historical beliefs, traditions, and celebrations associated with birthdays are examined. Included are an astrological chart, colors, flowers, and birthstones for each month of the year.

A collection of poems, both humorous and serious, illustrated with full-color drawings.

Hopkins, Lee Bennett, selector. *Happy Birthday.* Illustrated by Hilary Knight. Simon & Schuster, 1991.

An anthology of poems depicting a child's birthday from the anticipation of its coming through to the end of the day. Full-color illustrations by Knight, illustrator of the popular *Eloise*, enhance the volume.

Livingston, Myra Cohn. *Birthday Poems*. Illustrated by Margot Tomes. Holiday House, 1989.

Twenty-four original poems celebrate the many aspects of birthdays, including "Beach Birthdays," "Dinosaur Birthday," and "Bicycle Birthday."

Noble, Trinka Hales. *Jimmy Boa and the Big Splash Birthday Bash*. Illustrated by Steven Kellogg. Dial, 1989.

A fun romp describing Jimmy's birthday party at Sea Land, which turns out to be a big splash where everyone ends up in a large tank.

Rylant, Cynthia. *Birthday Presents*. Illustrated by Suçie Stevenson. Orchard, 1987.

A five-year-old girl listens as her mother and father recount her previous birthday celebrations.

Seuss, Dr. *Happy Birthday to You!* Random House, 1959.

The Great Birthday Bird of Katroo is on hand to help celebrate the Day of Days. Seuss' amusing verse and illustrations will delight any birthday child.

Williams, Vera B. *Something Special for Me*. Greenwillow, 1983.

Rosa chooses a special birthday present to buy with the coins her mother and grandmother have saved—a used accordion "waiting . . . to make songs come out of it."

Zolotow, Charlotte. *Mr. Rabbit and the Lovely Present*. Illustrated by Maurice Sendak. Harper, 1962.

This 1963 Caldecott Honor Book tells of Mr. Rabbit, who helps a young girl find a lovely present for her mother's birthday.

Learning About Families

Children can be asked how far back they can trace family origins. Parents and grandparents can aid in such a project by telling children when and where they were born. The information garnered can be the basis of creating a Family Tree.

Books can aid children in tracing their roots as well as finding out about family structures that are common in the 1990's; they can also spark a variety of written and oral language activities.

Me and My Family Tree, a Let's-Read-and-Find-Out Science Book by Paul Showers, illustrated by Don Madden (Harper, 1978), discusses in easy-to-read terms the principles of genetics and heredity.

The Great Ancestor Hunt: The Fun of Finding Out Who You Are by Lila Perl (Clarion, 1989) is a book for middle and upper graders to inspire their personal histories. The volume, illustrated with over forty photographs and drawings, includes period advertisements and an illustrated time-line.

Several choice titles that portray today's ever-changing family life-styles include:

Bradley, Buff. *Where Do I Belong? A Kid's Guide to Stepfamilies.* Harper, 1982.

For middle to upper graders, this volume deals with divorce and remarriage, and offers advice and resources for readjustment.

Brown, Laurene Krasney, and Marc Brown. *Dinosaurs Divorce: A Guide to Changing Families.* Little, Brown, 1986.

Like people in the twentieth century, if dinosaurs got married they would undoubtedly cope with divorce, too. In this reassuring book, the problems of divorce are tackled head-on and possible ways of handling them suggested. The text is illustrated with full-color, cartoon-style pictures.

Christiansen, C. B. *My Mother's House, My Father's House.* Illustrated by Irene Trivas. Atheneum, 1989.

A child travels back and forth between two different houses. From Monday through Thursday, she lives in her mother's house, from Friday through Sunday at her father's. Although she loves both parents, she dreams of the day she will live in one house seven days a week—without needing a suitcase!

Jenness, Aylette. *Families: A Celebration of Diversity, Commitment, and Love.* Houghton, 1990.

The lives of seventeen families from around the United States, some with step relationships, divorced parents, gay parents, foster siblings, and other diverse family components are depicted. Illustrated with black-and-white photographs by the author, this book was the basis for a traveling exhibition by the Children's Museum in Boston, Massachusetts.

Livingston, Myra Cohn. *There Was a Place and Other Poems.* McElderry Books, 1988.
A collection of verses written from the perspective of children, many from dysfunctional families.

Perry, Patricia, and Marietta Lynch. *My Mommy and Daddy Are Divorced.* Dial, 1978.
Ned, whose parents have just divorced, learns to cope with his new family situation. Illustrated with black-and-white photographs.

Simon, Norma. *All Kinds of Families.* Illustrated by Joe Lasker. Whitman, 1976.
A book that explores how families vary in make-up and life-styles.

Much research in the area of self-concept is still desperately needed. The sequence through which self-image is developed is not completely known or understood. However, the devices described above are practical means of helping children to see themselves more clearly. They do not involve the expenditure of vast sums of money for fancy hardware or equipment; they are techniques that build upon the natural endowments granted to all children—a name, a birthday, an image, a self! The educator, working in cooperation with other teachers, a school system, a neighborhood, or parents, can create endless possibilities for strengthening the growth potential of children. Perhaps if we try, implement, and elaborate upon some of the ideas presented here, children will acquire more positive views of themselves and will not pose such questions as that of the Native American youngster who asked plaintively: "Teacher, who am I?"

PART TWO

Journeys to the Land of Books
Children's Literature

GOOD BOOKS, GOOD TIMES!
Lee Bennett Hopkins

> Good books.
> Good times.
> Good stories.
> Good rhymes.
> Good beginnings.
> Good ends.
> Good people.
> Good friends.
> Good fiction.
> Good facts.
> Good adventures.
> Good acts.
> Good stories.
> Good rhymes.
> *Good* books.
> *Good* times.

There was an old woman
Who lived in a shoe.
She had so many children,
She didn't know what to do . . .

****

Little Miss Muffet
Sat on a tuffet
Eating her curds and whey . . .

****

Most children and adults recognize that these rhymes are from the favorite mother in all literature—Mother Goose. Mother Goose, long an important figure in our literary heritage, has been dealt with in every conceivable way in books for children. Since 1697, when Charles Perrault published a collection of nursery tales entitled *Histoires ou Contes du Temps Passé* (*Stories or Tales of Long Ago*) and captioned a picture on the frontispiece "Contes de Ma Mère l'Oye" ("Tales of Mother Goose"), this character has appeared and reappeared in every major language. Countless English and American editions have been published year after year and have been illustrated by the top artists in the field of children's literature. Illustrators such as Marguerite de Angeli, Arnold Lobel, Wendy Watson, and Tomie de Paola have interpreted the rhymes of old, all in their own unique styles.

This is one of the wonderful qualities about classic

books for children—they rarely go out of date. Many of the books written and published during the nineteenth and early twentieth centuries are more popular now than they were when they first appeared. Consider this list:

1843 — *A Christmas Carol* by Charles Dickens
1846 — *The Fairy Tales of Hans Christian Andersen*
1865 — *Alice's Adventures in Wonderland* by Lewis Carroll
1869 — *Little Women* by Louisa May Alcott
1884 — *Huckleberry Finn* by Mark Twain
1900 — *The Wizard of Oz* by L. Frank Baum
1902 — *The Tale of Peter Rabbit* by Beatrix Potter
1904 — *Peter Pan* by Sir James M. Barrie.

These are just a few of the many books that were milestones of literature. Think of how many millions of children have come to know and love characters such as Tom Thumb, Alice and her weird and fanciful friends, Huck and Tom, Dorothy and her companions who travel down the Yellow Brick Road, Peter Pan, Wendy, and Tinkerbell. Think of the millions of youngsters who have shared heartaches with the March family when Beth dies at a young age, or those who have felt compassion for the Ugly Duckling.

A host of contemporary books has many of the same qualities as the literary classics above. One can find more memorable characters and situations in books than in any other media.

Where else could you find such fantastic characters

as Mary Poppins, the English nanny who can fly with an umbrella, created by P. L. Travers (Harcourt, 1934), or Fern, a farmer's young daughter who names a pet pig Wilbur and pushes him around in a doll buggy in E. B. White's *Charlotte's Web* (Harper, 1952)?

Although most characters in books for children are fictitious, people such as the beautiful Miyax who survives the perils of the Alaskan tundra in *Julie of the Wolves* by Jean Craighead George (Harper, 1972), or Sarah and her new family in *Sarah, Plain and Tall* by Patricia MacLachlan (Harper, 1985), really do seem to live and breathe!

Pick up any travel brochure. Look through it carefully. Certainly none of the real places on any of the world's continents sound as exciting as the places one can travel to in the world of children's literature. Such places as Prydain, created by Lloyd Alexander, where Cauldron-Born creatures live on even after death, or the village of Instep, brought to life by Natalie Babbitt in *Kneeknock Rise* (Farrar, 1970), whose inhabitants are cast in a spell by the Megrimum that lurk on the mist-wreathed peak of Kneeknock Rise. These sites whet one's appetite for adventure far more than a trip to Paris or London would.

In books for children, animals are more extraordinary than any real animal could ever hope to be. There are the unforgettable horses—Anna Sewell's Black Beauty, and Walter Farley's Black Stallion and Man O' War; the Damon Runyon–type animals—Chester Cricket, Tucker

Mouse, and Harry Cat in George Selden's *The Cricket in Times Square* (Farrar, 1960); even wild things, characters by Maurice Sendak, who have been adored by children and adults since 1963, when *Where the Wild Things Are* (Harper) first appeared.

Tiny chuckles and hearty laughs are to be found in children's books. Beverly Cleary's adventures of Ramona and Henry Huggins, or Harriet the Spy, Louise Fitzhugh's feisty character, spark riotously funny reading. There are quiet moments to sigh over and silent tears to shed, too, when Sounder crawls under the cabin to die in William Armstrong's *Sounder* (Harper, 1969), when a young girl is sent to endure harsh years in a Siberian work camp in Esther Hautzig's *The Endless Steppe* (Harper, 1968), or when the proud Amos Fortune is stripped of his dignity and made a slave, depicted in Elizabeth Yates' *Amos Fortune, Free Man* (Dutton, 1950).

People—book people—have given us a wide world to enjoy—a world reflecting the complexities of the real world in which we live.

Questions often asked by adults include: What do children *look for* in books? What *interests* them? What do I do when a child says, "Give me a *good book* to read!"?

Children and adults seek the same qualities in books—they want a book that has a strong plot and plenty of action. They want to read a story they can identify with, one with realistic, true-to-life characters. Children want books that enable them to understand the different cultures and customs they encounter in life. This need can be met by many of the thousands of books that roll off publishing presses annually.

Give and Get the Very Best

Certain styles of writing appeal to children; they often enjoy books written by the same author or books of the same type. It is not uncommon for children to read series after series of books or collections of books by one author. Many children know Dr. Seuss for his fanciful creations, Marguerite Henry for her exciting tales of horses, Paul Goble for his wondrous books reflecting Native American culture, Beverly Cleary for her characters who deal with the problems and pleasures of growing up. They ask for books by certain authors knowing that they will find something similar to what they read before, something that will be just right for them.

Although many children enjoy popular fad books, devouring title after title in a formulaic series, adults must take the lead in directing them to books of quality. Children's literature is cluttered with mediocre volumes. We must guide children in their reading preferences, introducing them to the excellent books they might otherwise miss. Many lives can be made richer and fuller if we know children and their books. If we do, we will have the right book, at the right time, for the child who asks, "Teacher, give me a *good* book!"

Pat Scales, a library media specialist at Greenville Middle School, Greenville, South Carolina, gives thoughtful insight when she writes: "Contrary to what many critics believe, today's students are capable of becoming discriminating readers. While they may often select fast-paced episodic stories to read for recreation, they are also open to studying novels that stretch their minds and expand their knowledge. Students like to search and explore, to compare and contrast, to discuss and create. Providing such experiences allows them to actively participate in their reading instruction; it also motivates them to share in the responsibility for their learning and encourages them to accept reading as an important and necessary part of their education" (*Book Links*, November 15, 1990, page 616).

The twentieth century is indeed the era of children's literature. There are more volumes being published now than ever before in history. With this explosion, however, teachers must know where to begin to look for material that will meet the needs of their students and how they can continue to gain information about new trends in books, new authors and illustrators, new materials. In a field that has become so rich so quickly, it is necessary to have a basic knowledge of where to look. The sources discussed below have been selected to aid you on your quest to give and get the very best.

Award-Winning Books

There are two major awards presented annually in the United States in the field of children's literature—the Newbery and the Caldecott awards.

The Newbery Award, named for the eighteenth-century English publisher and bookseller John Newbery, has been presented annually since 1922 to the author of "the most distinguished contribution to American literature for children published in the United States during the preceding year."

The Caldecott Award, named for Randolph Caldecott, the outstanding nineteenth-century English illustrator of children's books, has been presented annually since 1938 to the illustrator of "the most distinguished American picture book for children published in the United States during the preceding year."

Both awards, donated by the Frederick G. Melcher family, are given by a committee of the American Library Association. In addition to each award, an unspecified number of Honor Book citations are given.

Lists of these books can easily be obtained from your local public children's librarian. Many of these books are in school and public library collections. Children should be made aware of these annual award-winning volumes. Teachers should familiarize themselves with the titles and use them whenever an opportunity arises. A study of the United States will be greatly enriched with such Newbery Medal titles as Carol Ryrie Brink's

Caddie Woodlawn (Macmillan, 1935), Jean Craighead George's *Julie of the Wolves* (Harper, 1972), Patricia MacLachlan's *Sarah, Plain and Tall* (Harper, 1985), or Russell Freedman's *Lincoln: A Photobiography* (Clarion, 1987).

During the winter season, many discussions can grow out of Caldecott Medal titles such as *White Snow, Bright Snow* by Alvin Tresselt, illustrated by Roger Duvoisin (Lothrop, 1947), *The Big Snow* by Berta and Elmer Hader (Macmillan, 1948), *The Snowy Day* by Ezra Jack Keats (Viking, 1962), or *The Polar Express* by Chris Van Allsburg (Houghton, 1985).

To stretch young imaginations, William Pène du Bois' *The Twenty-One Balloons*, the 1948 Newbery Award–winner (Viking, 1947), or *Hey, Al!*, the 1987 Caldecott Award–winner by Arthur Yorinks, illustrated by Richard Egielski (Farrar, 1986) can be read over and over again. Various cultures can be explored in *Arrow to the Sun* by Gerald McDermott, the 1975 Caldecott Award–winner (Viking, 1974), or *Ashanti to Zulu: African Traditions* by Margaret Musgrove, illustrated by Leo and Diane Dillon, the 1977 Caldecott Award–winner (Dial, 1976).

More than ever before in the history of children's books, youngsters are being guided to choose what they feel are among the best books written, illustrated, and published for them. From Vermont to Hawaii, thousands of students participate each year by voting for their favorite titles.

Children's Literature Awards and Winners: A Directory of Prizes, Authors, and Illustrators, compiled by Dolores Blythe Jones (Gale, 1988, second edition), provides international coverage of over two hundred awards. Two such programs include the Dorothy Canfield Fisher Children's Book Award and the Nene Award.

The Fisher Award, first given in 1956–57, is cosponsored by the Vermont PTA and the State Department of Libraries to encourage Vermont children to read more and better books, to discriminate in choosing worthwhile books, and to honor one of the state's most distinguished literary figures. Annually, the children vote from a master list of thirty titles, narrowing the list to one winner.

The Nene Award has been presented annually since 1964 by Hawaiian school children in grades four through six who honor an author of the book receiving the greatest number of votes. The award is sponsored by the Children's Section of the Hawaii Library Association and the Hawaii Association of School Libraries.

If such programs do not exist in the area where you are teaching, you can encourage your students to create their own book awards. They can set criteria, make nominations, and then vote for the book they feel is best. Criteria can center around special themes or topics, fiction or nonfiction books, volumes of poetry, or books about special places or regions.

Many teachers, with the aid of library media specialists effectively use various genres to stimulate reading interests. For example, a fifth-grade class in Scarsdale, New York, was asked to read books dealing with fantasy during a one-month period. Booktalks were planned by the children, who shared titles they truly loved and wanted others to read. At the end of the month, each child cast a vote for the Fantasy of the Month. The class chose Alan Arkin's *The Lemming Condition* (Harper, 1975). A group of students then designed a scroll, which each class member signed, and sent it to the author in care of the publishing house. Several weeks later, a warm letter from the publishers stated that they had shared the news with Mr. Arkin, who was quite delighted.

A fourth-grade class in New York City chose "Urban Books" as a theme. After reading dozens of titles depicting the urban environment and discussing each one in terms of text and illustrations, the class decided to give an award to the most enjoyable book. A committee of artists designed a medal made of aluminum foil.

Each year in January, just prior to the American Library Association's announcements of the annual Newbery and Caldecott awards, many teachers stage a mock Newbery or Caldecott meeting in their classrooms, gathering together the books that are possible recipients—those that have received starred reviews in *School Library Journal*, *Booklist*, or *Horn Book* magazines.

Projects such as these get children to read many fine books and serve to spark true thinking.

Periodicals

In her article "Library Literature for Teachers" (*Language Arts*, March 1988), Anne Lundin, Assistant Curator of the de Grummond Children's Literature Research Collection at the University of Southern Mississippi, in Hattiesburg, Mississippi, states: "I come from a background of fifteen years in the English classroom and never knew that . . . reading the professional literature related to children's books is not the sole role of the librarian. It is a pleasure which belongs to all those who work with children, including parents and teachers."

To help you to be aware of the many resources offered to aid in keeping up, the periodicals listed below are those that offer reviews, critical articles, and ideas galore to help build excellent literature programs throughout the grades.

To familiarize yourself with these journals, ask a children's librarian to steer you toward them, or write for subscription information and sample copies. Few library budgets allow for subscriptions to all these periodicals; thus, after getting to know the philosophy behind each, you can decide what is best for you and your school or classroom needs.

Three of the journals with the largest circulations are *Booklist*, *The Horn Book*, and *School Library Journal*.

Booklist is published twice monthly, September

through June, and monthly in July and August, "to provide a guide to current print and nonprint materials worthy of consideration by small and medium-sized public libraries and school library media centers." In addition to reviews, specially prepared booklists are highlighted—for example, "Playing the Game: Sports Fiction"; "Picture Books with Historical Settings." For information write to the American Library Association.

The Horn Book, published six times a year, features articles on authors and illustrators, and reviews of recent books. In addition, each year acceptance speeches of award-winning authors, including the recipients of the Newbery and Caldecott awards, appear. For information write to The Horn Book, Inc.

School Library Journal: The Magazine of Children's, Young Adults', and School Librarians is a monthly publication. In addition to a multitude of reviews, there are scores of pertinent articles on literature, book-promotion strategies, interviews, and reviews of nonprint media. For information write to *School Library Journal*.

In addition to these, there are several most worthwhile publications that have strong, practical tie-ins with the elementary curriculum:

Book Links: Connecting Books, Librarians, and Classrooms, published bimonthly six times a year, is "dedicated to helping teachers and librarians find good books to use with children." Drawing from current titles and the "tried-and-true," the journal aids in the development of ideas for linking books together to support the curriculum and to make reading meaningful. First published in November 1990, premiere issues included sections such as "Book Strategies"—essays focusing on how to use one book or a group of books on a theme, and "Inside Story"—an in-depth look at how one book evolved, with comments from the author, a biographical sketch, and a list of related titles. For information write to the American Library Association.

Bulletin of the Center for Children's Books, published monthly except August, evaluates current titles, offering suggestions as to how books can be used for curricular use and developmental values. For information write to The University of Chicago Press.

CBC Features, a classroom bonanza from the Children's Book Council that appears two or three times a year, contains articles about news and events, and interviews with people in the publishing world. A wonderful aspect of this broadside is a section called "Materials Available" that provides listings of free and/ or inexpensive items to send away for (bookmarks by the packet, posters, biographies of authors and illustrators). A *one-time* handling fee puts you on this nonprofit organization's mailing list *forever!* You can get your students involved by having them write for the materials offered—a sound letter-writing experience. Most of the items, priced under $2.00 each if ordered in bulk, are wonderful for bulletin board displays, reading incentives, or for providing ideas for projects to use literature in the classroom. For information write to The Children's Book Council.

The CLA Bulletin, the journal of the Children's Literature Assembly of the National Council of Teachers of English (NCTE), appears three times a year with contributing articles from educators, authors, and critics, as well as reviews of new titles, news, and announcements. Recent issues have featured "Using Literature in the Classroom" and "A Focus on Folktales." For information write to NCTE.

The Five Owls, published bimonthly, is a creation of a group of children's literature enthusiasts from the Midwest "to encourage reading and literacy among young people by advocating books with integrity; those books that can be judged intelligent, beautiful, well-made and worthwhile in relation to books and literature in general." The newsletter contains special themed booklists, articles on various genres, interviews, and reviews of recent books. For information write to *The Five Owls*.

The Journal of the Children's Literature Council of Pennsylvania is published quarterly under the auspices of the Dauphin County Library System. Each issue contains informative articles as well as reviews of recent books. Past issues have included features such as "Intergenerational Programs" by Carol Eklund, offering exciting ways to spark studies about aging, followed by an "Intergenerational Bibliography" by Jane Compton, and articles on storytelling and the use of historical fiction. In support of the *Journal*, bookstores throughout the state and in Baltimore, Maryland, offer five- to ten-percent discounts on various purchases. For information write to: The Children's Literature Council of Pennsylvania.

The New Advocate, a quarterly journal devoted "to those involved with young people and their literature," features a wide variety of articles as well as a "Book Review Sampler" by M. Jean Greenlaw. Several contributions to past issues have been articles by authors Katherine Paterson, Lloyd Alexander, Gail E. Haley, and Myra Cohn Livingston. "In the Artist's Studio," a feature by Jane Yolen, focuses on the life-styles and work of prominent illustrators such as Charles Mikolaycak, Mordicai Gerstein, and Jane Dyer. For information write to Christopher-Gordon Publishers, Inc.

The Web, published three times annually, gives sound ideas on webbing all genres of children's books throughout the curriculum "to entangle you and your children with Wonderfully Exciting Books." In addition to book reviews and suggestions as to how books can be practically used, each issue includes a double-paged "web" centering on a particular theme. Recent issues have been designed around articles entitled "Exploring Mythology," "Dinosaurs and Digs," "Giants," and "Eats." This wonderfully exciting resource also includes in-depth teacher and student reactions to books—one of the few places where the voices of those who are truly using books on a daily basis can be heard. For information write to *The Web*.

Other Sources

Many newspapers feature special sections on children's books during Children's Book Week, which is usually celebrated during April and November each year. Encourage students to look for these special supplements. Bulletin-board displays can feature information clipped from them, and files of this material can be kept for future use.

If your local newspaper does not herald an event such as Children's Book Week, a group of students might write a letter to the editor suggesting its importance in this age of literature and literacy.

Individual publishing houses provide information about children's books, particularly new books. At least twice a year catalogs are distributed, giving the titles, annotations, prices, and grade levels of new volumes. To become acquainted with new authors and trends in publishing, ask to be placed on mailing lists and then browse through the catalogs you receive. Many publishing houses also distribute excellent material for classroom use, such as posters, book jackets, bookmarks, and information about authors and illustrators. *CBC Features* is one place where much of this free and/or inexpensive material is cited.

Bookstores and public and school libraries also provide material on books. Catalogs, special bibliographies, and book displays are usually available for teachers and parents to use and peruse.

Reading to Children

Children love to be read to. They like to sit and listen to stories, anecdotes, and tales of long ago. They love to laugh, cry, imagine, go on wild, carefree adventures. Any classroom teacher who has had the experience of sharing a chapter a day from an ongoing book knows how rich this time can be. All children should be read to every day. Five or ten minutes should be found and set aside for sharing the beautiful language that can be found in print. Books read aloud can awaken many interests, can encourage children to read more by themselves, and can aid in developing a taste for fine literature.

Many schools across the country, in addition to encouraging read-aloud times, have initiated Sustained Silent Reading Time (SSRT), or DEAR—Drop Everything And Read—popularized by Beverly Cleary in *Ramona Quimby, Age 8* (Morrow, 1981).

This is a time when everyone in the class, or in some places, an entire school, reads: everyone—from the principal to the custodian. The time allotment can be anywhere from five to ten minutes in lower grades to forty-five minutes in upper grades.

Teachers of early grades seem to read more readily to children. In preschool programs, in kindergarten, and in grades one through three, it seems as natural to read to children as it does to turn on the lights. Middle-grade students, however, are often neglected. Older boys and girls need this type of communication just as much as younger children do.

There are many excellent books to read to older children—many that they might miss if they are not read aloud. Complete stories, portions of books, even short descriptive passages can be shared. Parts of *Dear Mr. Henshaw*, the 1984 Newbery Award title by Beverly Cleary (Morrow, 1983); *The People Could Fly: American Black Folktales* by Virginia Hamilton, illustrated by Leo and Diane Dillon (Knopf, 1985); or *Matilda* by Roald Dahl (Viking, 1988) might be selected to whet appetites or just to acquaint children with selections of excellent prose.

Many children barely know what it is like to be read to. Many working parents cannot take the time to sit and read stories aloud; many cannot read well themselves. Their children, therefore, have very little opportunity to observe an adult family member engaged in reading activities. Teachers who regularly read to their classes several minutes a day can provide this important experience—one lacking in so many children's lives.

Read-Aloud Service Clubs

Read-Aloud Service Clubs are very successful with children. This project involves having older children read to younger children, developed so that kindergarten and first-, second-, and third-grade students may see readers in a somewhat intellectual role rather than in the role of hall guard, office monitor, or eraser cleaner. Teachers as well as children find this service one that is exciting and beneficial. Lower- and upper-grade teachers can hold meetings to initiate the clubs, setting aside a specific hour each week for children to participate in this activity, working out ways to give critical appraisal to the readers. Committees of teachers *and* students can be organized to select appropriate books to be used with young children.

The method is simple. A child in an upper grade is assigned to read or tell a story to a lower-grade class. Other children in the class can accompany the story-teller, implementing a demonstration with artwork, puppetry, creative dramatics, or audiovisual aids. An interesting sideline is that fifth and sixth graders who have reading difficulties can peruse easy-to-read books and materials without losing face. These children can participate in a Read-Aloud Service Club and contribute to it in many ways.

Teachers of the upper grades can plan practice sessions in their classrooms in which students read to one another and discuss the salient points of good storytelling. Charts can be made to illustrate such points as how to read a story effectively, how to pronounce words, how to use tone and pitch in one's voice, and ways in which readers might animate the particular story they choose to read. Charts can be posted to serve as constant reminders of what makes a good reader or teller of stories. The Read-Aloud Service Club is then ready to be launched within the school.

Many benefits evolve from this service—older children have the chance to renew acquaintances with favorite books, and they come to know fine contemporary volumes of recent vintage. It provides an incentive for going to the library, it encourages students to choose, review, and evaluate books for use with younger children, and it develops responsibility in everyone involved in the program.

Hundreds of books are shared, more are reviewed, and children of all ages, grade levels, and achievement levels profit from this unique service.

Storytelling

Storytelling is a most effective way of enriching the lives of children in the elementary grades and of leading them to books. Teachers who have a wide variety of stories up their sleeves can, at a moment's notice, shake cuffs and speak words that will enrapture their listeners. They can involve listeners in a tale of long ago or once upon a time. They can jolt the senses, stir imaginations, and provide young audiences with the literary heritage they so greatly deserve.

Storytelling is more difficult than reading aloud. Storytelling techniques must be mastered if a teacher is going to be effective. But once they are, rewards are paid off in contagious excitement, expressive faces, and cries of "Tell it over! Tell it over again!"

The guidelines below will help you on your storytelling quest:

1. Read the story you are going to tell to yourself until you are familiar with the action.
2. Tell the story aloud listening to your own voice, preferably using a tape recorder to note nuances, and to see how you might vary tone and pitch to make the story more dramatic.
3. Choose stories that *you* like to tell.

Often we can glean tips from hearing professional actors and storytellers reading stories. In recent years scores of books have been adapted on cassettes. Several to turn to include Judy Collins' narration of Hans Christian Andersen's *Thumbelina*, retold by Deborah Hautzig, illustrated by Kaarina Kaila (Random House, 1990); Mia Farrow's rendition of *Beauty and the Beast*, retold and illustrated by Mordicai Gerstein (Dutton, 1989); Katharine Hepburn's performances in *World of Stories* (Harper, 1988), which includes six classics: "Jack and the Beanstalk," "The Nightingale," "The Musicians of Bremen," "Beauty and the Beast," "The Emperor's New Clothes," and "Tattercoats."

Journals such as *Booklist* and *School Library Journal*, mentioned earlier in this chapter, can keep you abreast of what is currently being produced. *School Library Journal*, for example, has a monthly feature, "Audiovisual Review," containing critical evaluations of varied

media relating to various curricular needs, from literature and language arts to parent education and teacher
in-service programs.

For a better understanding of and appreciation for
Native American cultures and changes that are taking
place in them, children on several reservations have
been encouraged and helped to search out and read or
tell stories and legends from their own and other tribes.
Teachers can also encourage children to invite tribal
storytellers to come to school and tell stories and legends. With the permission of the storytellers, the sessions are taped for future use. Such programs can be
developed with children anywhere—from the Appalachian region to inner cities.

If children frequently hear many of the rich tales that
are available, they will be more apt to run to books to
find more and more. A resource to consult is *The
Family Story-Telling Handbook* by Anne Pellowski,
founder of the Information Center on Children's Cultures of the United States Commission for UNICEF, illustrated by Lynn Sweat (Macmillan, 1987). Subtitled
"How to Use Stories, Anecdotes, Rhymes, Handker-
chiefs, Paper, and Other Objects to Enrich Your Family
Traditions," the book offers a bibliography, additional
sources of good stories to tell, and a helpful listing of
storytelling events that take place in the United States,
Canada, Europe, and Asia. Other titles by the author are
*The Story Vine: A Source Book of Unusual and Easy-to-
Tell Stories from Around the World*, also illustrated by

Lynn Sweat (Macmillan, 1984) and *The World of Story-telling* (Wilson, revised edition, 1990).

Building Classroom Libraries

The classroom library can be the most important part of the learning environment when it contains books that meet the interests and needs of each individual child. And who knows such interests and needs better than the classroom teacher?

There are many ways to set up a classroom library; with a little effort, an exciting reading center can be developed. In one school where there was a lack of shelving, several teachers, with their students, set up a rolling library table. Books were placed on the table, which could be rolled around to various rooms to service individuals or groups of children. Books were changed frequently by a committee of children who served as roving librarians. This same technique can be employed in a single classroom utilizing a table on wheels to highlight special topics or themes such as Island Homes, Books in Spanish, Great Tastes in Literature, Poetry Parades, or Award-Winning Books.

In any classroom a reading corner can be planned. In addition to books, a table and chair may be in the corner, and a rug or pillows placed on the floor for comfort while browsing or relaxing. Artifacts might "advertise" a specific book; for example, a stuffed toy leopard next to a copy of *A Story, A Story: An African*

Tale by Gail E. Haley, the 1971 Caldecott Award winner (Atheneum, 1970); a toy spider to advertise *Anansi, the Spider: A Tale from the Ashanti* by Gerald McDermott, a 1973 Caldecott Honor Book (Holt, 1972); a toy train to highlight *The Polar Express* by Chris Van Allsburg, the 1986 Caldecott Award winner (Houghton, 1985); or a stuffed toy owl alongside *Owl Moon* by Jane Yolen, illustrated by John Schoenherr, the 1988 Caldecott Award winner (Philomel, 1987).

Logs of books children have read should appear somewhere in the classroom. One fourth-grade teacher utilizes a long piece of wood covered with brightly colored burlap as a House of Books. Children have envelopes with their names printed on them, and when a book is finished, they place in the envelope an index card listing the title, author, and their reactions. This provides a quick check of books read for both teachers and children.

Another idea used to decorate an Appalachian classroom was the construction of book scrolls. Children decorated long pieces of brown kraft paper and titled their scrolls "Sally's Book List," "Marilou's Memories," or "Jay Donald's Inventory." The scrolls were hung around the room; each time a child completed a book, the title, author and/or illustrator, and a one-sentence summary or illustration were added to the scroll.

In one classroom a teacher worked out a classroom library program that included a few books at a time. The books were listed in a column on a large chart; the children's names were written across the top. Boys and girls were encouraged to rate the books by color—blue for excellent, yellow for fair, green for good, or purple for poor. When several opinions appeared, the teacher discussed the books with the entire class. Those volumes that received favorable reviews were kept on the shelf; those the children did not enjoy were removed and replaced with new titles.

If children are encouraged to have a say as to what goes into *their* libraries, they will show more interest in reading and sharing books.

Paperback Books

Paperback books aid in building classroom libraries; their popularity has become a twentieth-century phenomenon, contributing enormously to educational programs. The low cost of paperbacks makes it easier to meet the individual needs of children, who have infinite varieties of interests. Children who cannot afford to own hardcover volumes, or children who do not have bookstores or public libraries in their immediate vicinity, have benefited from classroom book clubs organized in schools.

Although there are several paperback book clubs available through schools, two of the best are organized by Dell and Scholastic.

Dell has two paperback book clubs: The Trumpet Club for Primary Grades and The Trumpet Club for

Middle Grades. For information write to the specific book club at Dell.

Scholastic offers five clubs: Firefly for preschoolers, See-Saw for grades K–1, Lucky for grades 2–3, Arrow for grades 4–6, and TAB for junior high school students. For information write to Scholastic.

Both companies offer an impressive, broad-range list of titles, many by favorite children's authors such as Maurice Sendak, Ezra Jack Keats, Roald Dahl, and Betsy Byars, as well as a miscellany of original print and nonprint items.

Teachers should use these clubs with scrutiny, however. Too often a great deal of pulp appears on the lists including joke books, and poorly written popular series books and volumes featuring contemporary movie and television tie-ins.

In addition to Dell and Scholastic, most major publishers are now issuing their own backlist titles in paperback editions. For example, Farrar, Straus & Giroux, Inc. produces Sunburst Books; Dial, Pied Piper Books; Harper, Trophy Books; Harcourt, Voyager Books. Being placed on publisher's mailing lists to receive catalogs will keep you abreast of this constantly growing field.

With the surge of paperbacks, paperback bookshops are increasing in popularity in schools throughout the country, many operated by parent-teacher associations, by groups of children within the school, or by teachers.

Such shops can meet the following needs: children can find a greater range of reading material and can have a variety of books to select from, read, and own; teachers can suggest various titles to augment the school curriculum; and parents have the opportunity to buy high-quality books for their children.

In one area where children cannot afford to buy paperbacks, a group of parents has set up a unique buying plan called "Save for a Book." Children from the various grades come several times a week to an area where the bookshop is housed to deposit their savings. Each child is given a card on which the amount of money saved is recorded. Pennies, nickels, dimes, and quarters are given to the adults or students in charge, who keep records of the children's savings. When a child has saved enough, a book is selected, the card is handed in, and the child starts a new one.

This idea has worked effectively and has made it possible to put hundreds of books into hundreds of children's lives. Many children might never have the opportunity to secure their own books if it were not for a plan like this.

Another innovative idea to build up classroom and school libraries with high-quality paperbacks is to encourage Birthday Donations. Usually when a child has a birthday, parents send in cupcakes or pizza for the entire class. Schools across the country are asking parents to donate a paperback book, for far less than the cost of cupcakes or pizza.

I have initiated this practice in countless schools, with great results. A bookplate placed in a book donated by the birthday child is inscribed with his or her name, birthdate, and age:

THIS BOOK WAS GIVEN BY
MARIA EDWARDS
ON HER 9TH BIRTHDAY
APRIL 13, 1991

Think of the possibilities! If your school has two hundred students, two hundred new books per year will come into the school. In five years, *one thousand* books! The cupcakes and pizzas are quickly forgotten; the books will be around for years and years for children to read and enjoy. A committee of teachers, parents, librarians, and children can be formed to select titles for purchase. This is an inexpensive, meaningful way to build book collections.

Another idea that has worked successfully in many schools is setting up a Book Swap Shop, where children trade books they no longer want for books they haven't read.

Those wanting to trade books bring in as many titles as they want to swap in exchange. In one Vermont school alone, some five thousand books found new readers through this idea.

Reading is Fundamental (RIF), spearheaded by the late Margaret McNamara in 1966 as a nonprofit action program to make inexpensive books, mainly paperbacks, a way of life for all of America's children from age three through students of high school age, is now the largest reading-motivation program in the United States, with projects in all fifty states, the District of Columbia, Guam, the Virgin Islands, and Puerto Rico. RIF works effectively in many diverse settings—schools and libraries, hospitals, recreation centers, Native American Indian reservations, and public housing projects. In the fall 1989 issue of the "RIF Newsletter," for example, a report is given on an innovative exchange between children of textile workers and children living in shelters. A book-and-sock exchange began in Mount Airy, a town in the foothills of the Blue Ridge Mountains in North Carolina, when a group of textile-mill families called the Sock Readers Club joined with the Surry Country hosiery manufacturers to send 10,000 pairs of socks to RIF for distribution to children in Washington, D.C., homeless shelters and soup kitchens. In exchange, the children of the textile-mill workers received 1,000 books from RIF.

For information on a wide array of services and publications provided by this organization, write to RIF.

School and Public Libraries

One of today's greatest concerns is to entice children into the library, providing activities that will be stimulating and exciting, making them want to come to the library frequently.

Public libraries make books of all kinds available to everyone. They provide many services for parents, teachers, and children. Even in many small towns, collections of art prints, records, and videocassettes are circulated, storytelling programs are held, and foreign-language book and record collections are made available. Library lessons and tours for special groups can usually be arranged. In rural areas, bookmobiles—libraries that travel through communities containing rather complete revolving collections of adults' and children's books—are quite common. Local newspapers are good sources to check for special library programs.

Good school library programs are just as important. The school library should be one of the most popular rooms in the school building. Here is a place where children can go constantly for fun and learning. The role of the school librarian, or school media specialist, has rapidly changed. Today many school librarians provide teachers and parents with all types of excellent resources for children. Many run paperback book clubs or bookstores, or plan special activities for small groups or classes during the school day or in after-school programs.

The Pequenakonck Elementary School in North Salem, New York, planned an Author's Visit, inviting Arthur Yorinks to talk to students about his writing of such books as *Hey, Al!*, illustrated by Richard Egielski, the 1987 Caldecott Award–winning title (Farrar, 1986). The event was part of a "Winter Celebration of Reading."

Each February is "I Love to Read" month in Waseca, Minnesota, culminating with a "Reading in the Store" program in which a variety of people—a fire fighter, dentist, school administrator—read to children at the Waseca Hy-Vee local grocery food chain at intervals throughout a designated day.

More than five hundred children and adults, many in costume, participated in a four-block Parade of Books through Doylestown, in Bucks County, Pennsylvania. Over four thousand books were carried in decorated wagons from the Melinda Cox Branch to the new Bucks County Library Center. Ribbons were awarded for the most imaginative costumes, which featured book characters such as Amelia Bedelia, the Cat in the Hat, and Clifford, the Big Red Dog.

Every child should be encouraged to obtain a library card—and use it. The many activities held in the library and frequent visits there can be valuable additional incentives for reading.

Stop for a moment, no matter what grade you are teaching, to find out how many of your students have library cards. Many teachers are shocked to find out how many students do *not* have library cards. One teacher reported that in her third-grade class only four out of thirty-three students had cards. Children cannot afford to miss the opportunity of going to the library. There may be several children in your own class who would welcome having these privileges but do not know how to go about securing a card. This is particularly true of children who move around a great deal or children newly arrived from other places. The few minutes it takes to help children obtain library cards will provide them a lifetime to reap the benefits of libraries.

Learning About Authors

It is always surprising to hear the misconceptions that children have about authors of books. Time and time again children say things like:

Do authors sleep?
I thought all authors were dead!
People who write books must be strange.
Do people who write books live in regular houses or in publishing houses?

If children are fed facts and anecdotes about the lives of authors, such misconceptions will disappear. There are many ways to acquaint children with authors. The

Junior Authors and Illustrators series, published since 1935 by H. W. Wilson, provides hundreds of short autobiographical and biographical sketches of renowned personalities in the field of children's literature.

Anne Commire has edited the series of reference books *Something About the Author: Facts and Figures About Authors and Illustrators of Books for Young People* (Gale). Biographical data, photographs of the authors, selected illustrations from their works, and data about their careers and writing are provided.

A newer collection, *Something About the Author Autobiographical Series* (Gale) contains autobiographical essays providing readers the chance to meet book creators "in person."

Horn Book, Inc., has published the acceptance speeches and biographical sketches of the Newbery and Caldecott medalists in four volumes: *Newbery Medal Books: 1922–1955* and *Caldecott Medal Books: 1938–1957*, both edited by Bertha Mahoney Miller and Elinor Whitney Field; and *Newbery and Caldecott Medal Books: 1956–1965,* and *Newbery and Caldecott Medal Books: 1966–1975*, edited by Lee Kingman. The books are a rich source of information for all who use these award-winning books in their literature programs.

Additional reference books are always being added. Due to the large number of volumes and their high cost, it is not likely that school library centers, or even small public libraries, will have all these books. Seek them out in large public library collections. You might ask a local librarian to discuss such volumes with students so they will know that they exist and be encouraged to use them.

Many publishing houses provide fact sheets about their authors and will send material for classroom use. Various journals and popular magazines often feature interviews or articles about authors that you can clip and file for future use.

In recent years there have been several autobiographies written by popular authors. Among others, they include:

Cleary, Beverly. *A Girl From Yamhill: A Memoir.* Morrow, 1988.

Cleary, née Beverly Atlee Bunn, recounts her youth growing up in the 1920's. Black-and-white photographs illustrate this autobiography of one of America's best-loved authors.

Dahl, Roald. *Boy* (1984) and *Going Solo* (1986) both Farrar.

The popular creator of modern classics (*Charlie and the Chocolate Factory, James and the Giant Peach, Matilda*) entertains readers with his exciting, offbeat life adventures and misadventures.

Foreman, Michael. *War Boy: A Country Childhood* Little, Brown, 1989.

The acclaimed British illustrator reminisces about his

wartime childhood during the 1940's in Pakefield, a fishing village on the Suffolk Coast. The volume is lavishly illustrated in a variety of art media.

A collective paperback volume, *Speaking for Ourselves: Autobiographical Sketches by Notable Authors of Books for Young Adults*, compiled and edited by Donald F. Gallo (NCTE, 1990) features eighty-seven well-known American and English authors, all of whom provide brief insights into their lives and work. Although the book is geared to young adult readers, many of the authors featured have written books for all grade levels—for example, Lloyd Alexander, Jean Craighead George, Judy Blume, and Jane Yolen.

Writing letters to authors can be a rewarding language-arts experience for children. One of the funniest and most charming letters I ever received was from a fifth-grade girl from Florida. She wrote:

> Dear Hopkins, Lee Bennett, Ed.,
>   I love your books. I can't think of my favorite one but I think that you are a good author and you write good books. I have two favrite authers in this whole wide world you and Judy blume but I wrote to you because I didn't have her address. . . .

It did not bother me at all that her spelling, punctuation, and capitalization were a tad off, nor that her greeting read "Dear Hopkins, Lee Bennett, Ed." It did take some time, however, to figure out what the "Ed." part meant, until I realized the student must have looked my name up in a card catalog, where "ed." stands for "editor"—editor of anthologies.

Since I *always* answer children's letters, I answered hers—but, I did *not* send her Judy Blume's address!

Teachers who encourage children to write letters to authors should know about several DOs and DON'TS.

DOs

1. Children should send letters to authors in care of their publishing houses. The publishers will forward the letters to the authors. Let children know that this process takes time. Sometimes several months can elapse between the time the child writes a letter and the time an author receives it. Popular authors such as Judy Blume, Beverly Cleary, and Shel Silverstein receive thousands of letters each year, making it impossible for them to answer each and every letter they receive. Some publishers send attractive brochures or printed messages, which should satisfy students.

2. Do encourage children to write legibly and to include their return addresses, including ZIP codes. I have received letters from children where, try as I might, I cannot decipher a first or last name. At times, I have even received letters signed something like "Christine T." or find that extra numbers are added to ZIP codes. I am always a bit sorry when my letters are returned from a post office marked "Insufficient Address," thinking that somewhere some child or teacher is blaming me for not writing back.

3. Do have children write from the heart. An excellent, insightful, poignant discussion of children writing let-

ters to authors can be found in Beverly Cleary's 1984 Newbery acceptance speech in *Newbery and Caldecott Medal Books: 1976–1985.* I would encourage every teacher to read this essay before turning children loose to engage in this type of letter-writing experience.

4. *Always* have students enclose a self-addressed, stamped envelope—*always!*

DON'Ts

1. Don't encourage children to write to dead authors! Although they might receive a reply from the publishing house, they will not receive a letter from the author! It is unbelievable how many children write letters to deceased authors—everyone from Sir Walter Scott to Scott O'Dell! Encourage students to find out if the author is alive by looking in reference volumes.

2. Don't have children send "class letters" in which every child in the room writes the same thing. Too often authors receive packets of such letters where each child states something like "Your book was interesting." *What* book? *Why* was it "interesting?" These packages usually leave authors cold, wondering if for the children this "experience" was only a meaningless letter-writing experience.

3. Don't have children ask authors for copies of their books. Sometimes I envision children thinking that authors sit amongst stacks of their books, towering to the ceiling, just waiting to send them off to someone. No authors I know have tons or even several of their own books to give away. When an author writes a book, he or she is usually given no more than ten copies, which

are used judiciously. After that, they have to *buy* copies, just like anyone else.

4. Don't have children ask questions such as "Where were you born? What was your first book? Can you give me some tips on writing?" Answers to such questions can be found in reference volumes.

In the article "Write as Though You Were Talking to Me: Kids, Letters, and Writers," (*English Journal*, March 1990), Norma Fox Mazer states:

> To help your students find their own voices, I strongly recommend that you encourage the expression of thoughts about a book that spring from inside the reader, rather than from a desire to score an A. To this end, discourage comments that arise lifelessly from no more than the need to fill space, including the dreaded regurgitation of plots. A short, brisk, truly felt letter is far more effective than a two-page robotic exercise.

Children would hear this sentiment from most authors.

Having an author visit a school or classroom can also be a rewarding event. Although an author's visit is an exciting event for all, it does take a great deal of preparation, planning, and budgeting for such an event to occur. A budget must include the author's travel costs, hotel, meals, and an honorarium, which varies greatly—from several hundred dollars to several thousand dollars.

You will need to set a date for an appearance— anywhere from several months to a year or more in advance. The author should be contacted through the publishing house, which will aid in making the initial contact with the author, arrange for travel, and provide you with guidelines for ordering the author's books for autographing.

Useful guidelines and practical suggestions are offered in the paperback volume *How To Capture Live Authors and Bring Them to Your Schools* by David Melton (Landmark, 1986).

The next best thing to authors' visits is to see them in person on videocassettes. The listing below offers programs on videocassettes featuring authors and illustrators discussing their work habits and interests, and in many cases showing them in their home environs. Each tape runs between thirteen and twenty-five minutes; for complete information on sale, rental, and/or preview, along with costs, write to the various producers for their catalogues.

Jim Aronsky: "Wonders of Nature: Drawing and Writing with Jim Aronsky." Silver Burdett.

Norman Bridwell: "The World of Norman Bridwell, Featuring Clifford, the Big Red Dog." Scholastic.

Marc Brown: "Meet Marc Brown." American School Publishers.

Ashley Bryan: "Meet Ashley Bryan: Story teller, Artist, Writer." American School Publishers.

Eve Bunting: "A Visit with Eve Bunting." Clarion.

Betsy Byars: "Stage Talk: An Interview with Betsy Byars on Character Development." Silver Burdett.

Roald Dahl: "The Author's Eye." American School Publishers.

Russell Freedman: "A Visit with Russell Freedman." Clarion.

Jean Fritz: "Meet Jean Fritz." Putnam.

Jean Craighead George: "Her Side of the Mountain: A Conversation with Jean Craighead George." Tim Podell Productions, Inc.; "The Adventurous Spirit: Jean Craighead George on Journal Writing." Silver Burdett.

Nikki Giovanni: "About Critiquing: Nikki Giovanni and Virginia Hamilton Share Their Opinions." Silver Burdett.

Mel Glenn: "Poetic Journey: Mel Glenn Focuses on Self-Expression." Silver Burdett.

Eloise Greenfield: "The Power of Dreams: Eloise Greenfield Connects Writing and Research." Silver Burdett.

Virginia Hamilton: See Nikki Giovanni above.

Lee Bennett Hopkins: "Good Conversation! A Talk with Lee Bennett Hopkins." Tim Podell Productions, Inc.

Karla Kuskin: "Good Conversation! A Talk with Karla Kuskin." Tim Podell Productions, Inc.

Madeleine L'Engle: "Madeleine L'Engle: StarGazer." Ishtar Films.

Lois Lowry: "A Visit With Lois Lowry." Houghton.

David Macaulay: "A Visit with David Macaulay." Houghton.

Patricia MacLachlan: "Patricia MacLachlan Explores Writing From Personal Experience." Silver Burdett.

James Marshall: "A Visit with James Marshall." Houghton.

Ann McGovern: "Good Conversation! A Talk with Ann McGovern." Tim Podell Productions, Inc.

Phyllis Reynolds Naylor: "Good Conversation! A Talk with Phyllis Reynolds Naylor." Tim Podell Productions, Inc.

Scott O'Dell: "A Visit with Scott O'Dell." Houghton.

Katherine Paterson: "The Author's Eye." American School Publishers.

Bill Peet: "A Visit with Bill Peet." Houghton.

Jerry Pinkney: "Meet the Caldecott Illustrator." American School Publishers.

Robert Quackenbush: "Dear Mr. Quackenbush" and "The Story of George Washington." Quackenbush Studios.

Cynthia Rylant: "Meet the Newbery Author." American School Publishers.

Dr. Seuss: "Who's Dr. Suess? Meet Ted Geisel." American School Publishers.

Elizabeth George Speare: "A Visit with Elizabeth George Speare." Houghton.

Nancy Willard: "Good Conversation! A Talk with Nancy Willard." Tim Podell Productions, Inc.

Jane Yolen: "One Misty Morning: Jane Yolen Talks About Observing and Writing." Silver Burdett.

The California Reading Association makes available a series of "Author Video Tapes." Each tape includes interviews with three authors, a segment in which students ask the authors questions based on their books, and the authors reading excerpts from one of their works. The various tapes span grade levels—for example, Tape II, for primary grades, includes Eve Bunting, Ruth Heller, and James Marshall; Tape I, for middle grades, highlights Lois Duncan, Zilpha Keatley Snyder, and Ted Taylor. For a descriptive listing on the series write to CRA Author Video Tapes.

Undoubtedly the future will bring more such programs for use in school and library programs.

Happy Birthday, Dear Author

Many language-arts activities can be sparked by celebrating the birthday of a favorite author or illustrator of children's books.

A bulletin-board display can highlight the celebration by posting a photograph of the personality, his or her birthdate, and a listing of books.

A committee of children can set out to do research on the life of the featured author. Story hours can include reading aloud specific books or chapters from them.

Here is a selected listing of author and illustrator birthdates. If the birthdates of your children's favorite book creators do not appear, have the children add their names to the list.

JANUARY
 2 Isaac Asimov
   Jean Little
 3 Joan Walsh
     Anglund
   Carolyn Haywood
   J.R.R. Tolkien
 4 Jakob Grimm
 6 Carl Sandburg
 9 Clyde Robert Bulla
11 Mary Rodgers

12 Clement Hurd
   Charles Perrault
13 N. M. Bodecker
   Michael Bond
16 Robert Lipsyte
17 John Bellairs
18 A. A. Milne
21 Vera B. Williams
22 Blair Lent
   Brian Wildsmith
26 Charles Mikolaycak

27 Henry Allard
   Lewis Carroll
   Jean Merrill
29 Bill Peet
30 Lloyd Alexander
31 Gerald McDermott

FEBRUARY
 1 Langston Hughes
 7 Laura Ingalls Wilder
10 Stephen Gammell
   E. L. Konigsburg
11 Jane Yolen
12 Judy Blume
15 Norman Bridwell
16 Nancy Ekholm Burkert
   Mary O'Neill
19 Louis Slobodkin
24 Wilhelm Grimm
25 Frank Bonham
   Cynthia Voigt
27 Uri Shulevitz

MARCH
 2 Leo Dillon
   Dr. Seuss
 4 Meindert de Jong
11 Wanda Gág
   Ezra Jack Keats
12 Virginia Hamilton
13 Dorothy Aldis
   Diane Dillon
   Ellen Raskin

14 Marguerite de Angeli
17 Lilian Moore
20 Lois Lowry
26 Robert Frost
28 Byrd Baylor

APRIL
 2 Hans Christian
   Andersen
 3 Washington Irving
 8 Trina Schart Hyman
12 Beverly Cleary
   Hardie Gramatky
13 Marguerite Henry
   Lee Bennett Hopkins
19 Jean Lee Latham
22 William Jay Smith
23 William Shakespeare
24 Evaline Ness
26 Patricia Reilly Giff
27 Ludwig Bemelmans
28 Lois Duncan

MAY
 5 Leo Lionni
 7 Nonny Hogrogian
 8 Milton Meltzer
 9 James M. Barrie
   Eleanor Estes
   William Pène du Bois
10 Margaret Wise Brown
11 Zilpha Keatley Snyder
12 Edward Lear

14 George Selden
15 L. Frank Baum
17 Eloise Greenfield
18 Lillian Hoban
   Irene Hunt
19 Tom Feelings
22 Arnold Lobel
23 Scott O'Dell
31 Elizabeth Coatsworth
   Beni Montresor

JUNE
 1 James Daugherty
 2 Paul Galdone
 3 Anita Lobel
 6 Verna Aardema
   Peter Spier
   Nancy Willard
 7 Gwendolyn Brooks
   Nikki Giovanni
10 Maurice Sendak
14 Laurence Yep
18 Chris Van Allsburg
24 Leonard Everett
   Fisher
   John Ciardi
25 Eric Carle
26 Robert Burch
   Walter Farley
   Lynd Ward
   Charlotte Zolotow
27 Lucille Clifton
30 David McPhail

JULY
 2 Jean Craighead George
11 E. B. White
   James Stevenson
13 Marcia Brown
   Ashley Bryan
14 Peggy Parish
16 Arnold Adoff
   Richard Egielski
17 Karla Kuskin
19 Eve Merriam
28 Natalie Babbitt
   Beatrix Potter

AUGUST
 1 Gail Gibbons
 6 Matt Christopher
   Barbara Cooney
 7 Betsy Byars
 9 Jose Aruego
10 Margot Tomes
11 Joanna Cole
   Don Freeman
   Alice Provensen
15 Brinton Turkle
16 Beatrice Schenk de
   Regniers
17 Myra Cohn Livingston
19 Ogden Nash
21 X. J. Kennedy
   Arthur Yorinks
28 Roger Duvoisin
   Virginia Lee Burton

30 Donald Crews

SEPTEMBER
 3 Aliki
 4 Syd Hoff
 5 Paul Fleischman
 8 Michael Hague
   Jack Prelutsky
 9 Aileen Fisher
13 Roald Dahl
   Else Holmelund Minarik
14 John Steptoe
15 William Armstrong
   Tomie de Paola
   Robert McCloskey
16 H. A. Rey
17 Paul Goble
24 Harry Behn
   Felice Holman
30 Alvin Tresselt

OCTOBER
 3 Natalie Savage Carlson
 7 Susan Jeffers
10 James Marshall
11 Russell Freedman
13 Katherine Paterson
14 Lois Lenski
19 Ed Emberley
26 Steven Kellogg
29 Valerie Worth

NOVEMBER
 1 Hilary Knight

   Symeon Shimin
 4 Gail E. Haley
14 William Steig
15 David McCord
   Daniel Manus Pinkwater
16 Jean Fritz
   Leo Politi
21 Elizabeth George Speare
   Isaac Bashevis Singer
24 Carlo Collodi
25 Marc Brown
28 Tomi Ungerer
   Ed Young
29 Louisa May Alcott
   Madeleine L'Engle
   C. S. Lewis
30 Margot Zemach

DECEMBER
 1 Jan Brett
 2 David Macaulay
 4 Munro Leaf
 5 Christina G. Rossetti
 6 Elizabeth Yates
13 Leonard Weisgard
14 Marylin Hafner
16 Marie Hall Ets
19 Eve Bunting
24 Feodor Rojankovsky
28 Carol Ryrie Brink
29 Molly Bang
30 Rudyard Kipling
   Mercer Mayer

Sharing Literature Through Experiences

Whole-language and literature-based reading programs are concepts of teaching that gained popularity in the late 1980's and continue to be a trend of the 1990's; such innovations have sparked more and more sharing of literature through hands-on experiences.

Teachers who believe in whole-language approaches to reading create classroom environments in which children are immersed in language, believing that students learn to read *by* reading, learn to write *by* writing, and learn to love books *by* loving them!

Although new terms have been used for such an approach, many seasoned educators have been "whole language" advocates from their earliest days of their careers.

Whatever the type of learning situation that is set up for students, you will find that literature can be shared in many ways. The important thing about the meaningful mesh of literature into the curriculum is that the experiences provided should be meaningful ones—those that children enjoy taking part in, those that grow naturally from their love of books. Forced book reports telling "the part I like best" or "what the book means to me" can be terribly dull. Children can love a book without analyzing it to death and without always writing about it. The written book report is a rather closed avenue of communication—the child writes something, the teacher reads it, and that is usually the end of it. For children to finish a book they have loved and to write "the book is about . . ." or "the part I liked best . . ." is a tragic waste. It is like going into a garden filled with magnificent flowers and smelling only one, or going to an action-packed circus to look at only one ring!

The more opportunities children have to be creative, the more they will create. Provide children with hands-on experiences, give them the chance to discover their abilities, and stand aside—let them grow!

Mapping Books

Maps of a city, state, continent, or the world can be posted in the classroom to pinpoint places where stories in children's literature occur. Pins with strings attached can show, for example, Wisconsin, where *Caddie Woodlawn* by Carol Ryrie Brink (Macmillan, 1935) takes place; New York City, the setting of E. L. Konigsburg's *From the Mixed-Up Files of Mrs. Basil E. Frankweiler* (Atheneum, 1967); or Boston, the setting for Robert McCloskey's *Make Way for Ducklings* (Viking, 1941). Perhaps a state where someone in a biography lived or died might be highlighted. Where fictitious places are key points in books, have the class members create original maps. Encourage them to let their imaginations soar as they map out the Yellow Brick Road in *The Wizard of Oz*, by L. Frank Baum, or *Rabbit Hill* by Robert Lawson (Viking, 1944), for nowhere will they find such magical places on a conventional map.

Elizabeth Dodd, a remedial teacher in South Bound Brook, New Jersey, utilized this idea with fifth graders in a folk-story unit. A large map of the United States was placed on a bulletin board. On a table underneath the bulletin board she put cutout footprints made from construction paper. In a letter she reported:

> As the kids got involved in reading stories about such American folk heroes as Captain Stormalong, Paul Bunyan, and Pecos Bill, they covered the United States with trails. Each time they read a story about different regional heroes, they put up a footprint on the map signed with their name, the character's name, the book title, and the author. It soon became a contest to see how quickly they could cross the country. Without their knowing it, their reading skills rapidly shot up!

Literature Newsletter

A bulletin-board display can be utilized to develop a Literature Newsletter modeled after a newspaper. Children can decide what columns or features they would like on the board; a rotating editorial staff can periodically change the news. This device is a good one for highlighting interesting events in books. After reading a book, a child can write a brief statement about a character or event and give it to the proper editor. Headlines might read:

MAX RETURNS
From *Where the Wild Things Are*

A lost-and-found item or a society note might be given to the feature editor:

LOST

Three Little Mittens by Three Little Kittens
Reward. Contact Mother Cat.

****

SOCIETY

Mr. March returned from the Civil War. Jo, Beth, Amy, and Meg, his daughters, planned a welcome-home party. You can read about it in *Little Women*.

A sports item could be handed to the sports editor:

BASEBALL LEGEND
ROBERTO CLEMENTE
BECOMES THE FIRST LATIN-AMERICAN PLAYER
TO BE ADMITTED TO THE BASEBALL HALL OF
FAME
Read about this All-Time Hero in
The Story of Roberto Clemente by Jim O'Connor

News items can be illustrated, or book jackets can accompany the stories. A literature bulletin board provides the child a method for reviewing books frequently, easily, and creatively.

Instant Reaction Card File

Children can be encouraged to record on index cards their instant reactions to the books they read. Young children or children who have difficulty writing can *tell* the teacher what they think about a book. The teacher, acting as scribe, can write down individual comments. Other children can write their own reactions to books they read. These cards can be filed in a small box, and can, at a glance, tell the teacher the types of books the children are reading and how many books they have completed. In this way overstructured book reports can be avoided, and the time usually spent on their preparation can be used for more creative ways of sharing literature. The samples below show two children's instant reactions:

I read *Straight Hair, Curly Hair* by Paul Showers and I liked it because I never knew anything about hair and I was amazed to find out all the things you can do with hair and I did them. And I know why my hair is curly, not straight, now.

Third grader

The Story of My Life by Helen Keller is the most beautiful book I have ever read. Even when I think about Helen's life, I get goose flesh bumps. I loved the book, and I loved the way it was written. I am going to read it again this summer.

Sixth grader

What more could meaningfully be said, or how much better could they have expressed themselves, if either child had worked longer on these reactions?

Descriptive Passage Portals

An effective technique used in several schools is a Descriptive Passage Portal. Teachers place a large brown envelope near the door and encourage children to contribute cards on which they have written favorite passages from their readings. When the children line up for gym period, to walk to the auditorium for a special event, or to go home, a child is selected to reach in and read (or have the teacher read) a passage submitted by a student:

> The barn was very large. It was very old. It smelled of hay and it smelled of manure. It smelled of the perspiration of tired horses and the wonderful sweet breath of patient cows. It often had a sort of peaceful smell—as though nothing bad could happen ever again in the world. (From *Charlotte's Web* by E. B. White, Harper, 1952.)

****

> Miyax pushed back the hood of her sealskin parka and looked at the Arctic sun. It was a yellow disc in a lime-green sky, the colors of six o'clock in the evening and the time when the wolves awoke. Quietly she put down her cooking pot and crept to the top of a dome-shaped frost heave, one of the many earth buckles that rise and fall in the crackling cold of the Arctic winter. (From *Julie of the Wolves* by Jean Craighead George, Harper, 1972.)

These above passages take only seconds to read. They provide children with ideas for the book-to-take-next from the library shelf, offer extraordinary language, and give contributors a wonderful feeling of pride and satisfaction when *their* descriptive passages are read before passing through the portal.

Combining Books With Art Experiences

Books can be shared through a variety of art experiences. After students have perused different types of bookmarks, turn them loose to create their own.

Several slogans the Children's Book Council has used to promote Book Week programs include: "Any Time, Any Place, Any Book"; "Wish Upon a Book"; "Good Books, Good Times!"; and "Gone Readin'."

After discussing these slogans with students encourage them to come up with their own ideas. They can then design individual bookmarks. The bookmarks can be used for a bulletin-board display, after which children can use them to mark the pages in the books they are currently reading.

Individuals, groups of children, or a whole class can prepare collages or murals. Brown kraft paper can be used as a background, with a variety of materials attached to it. The specific theme of a collage or mural should be decided upon by the class.

One fourth grade decided to depict the tea-party scene from *Alice's Adventures in Wonderland* by Lewis Carroll, and made a six-foot-long mural. Alice, the Mad

Hatter, and the March Hare were blown up to giant proportions; cloth was used for clothing, colored yarn for hair, and plastic toy dishes for the table setting; the background was painted in tempera, and the finished product was placed in the school hall for all the students to enjoy thoroughly.

Younger children could depict scenes from their favorite books on burlap. Characters and objects cut from paper or material can be applied to the burlap with thread or glue.

Constructing puppets of favorite book characters is another way of sharing literature. Children on every grade level can produce various types of puppets with great satisfaction. Simple drawings can be stapled to sticks or tongue depressors to obtain interesting effects. Large corks or Styrofoam balls can easily be turned into puppets by using thumbtacks for eyes, yarn for hair, and paper for noses and mouths. Sticks can be inserted into the base of the cork for movement. Original drawings can also be made and thumbtacked onto corks or Styrofoam. Papier-mâché, potatoes, paper bags, and socks are other items that can be used for puppet construction.

A good resource to consult on making puppets is *The Little Pigs' Puppet Book* by N. Cameron Watson (Little, Brown, 1990). This picture book, illustrated in full color, tells of three pig brothers who decide to put on a puppet play for their friends, creating everything from scratch—the puppets, script, stage scenery, programs, tickets, and refreshments. Detailed directions are given for making sock, tube, and jaw puppets. Though geared toward younger readers, a host of ideas for children of all ages are presented in this most worthwhile volume.

Puppets provide an excellent outlet for encouraging more effective speech. Children who are shy or who cannot speak English fluently often find it easier to speak through a puppet, for it is not they who are talking but the character whom the puppet represents.

Original book jackets can spark a great deal of creativity. Children can design their own jackets and display them next to the original ones designed by the publishing houses. They can also write an advertisement, a summary of the book, or a biographical sketch of the author for the jacket flap.

With the use of overhead projectors, child-made pictures are good media for sharing literature. In one fifth-grade classroom a child chose the classic Puerto Rican folktale *Perez and Martina*, retold by Pura Belpré, illustrated by Carlos Sanchez (Warne, 1961) and read his classmates the tale. Various children volunteered to draw scenes from the book without seeing the original drawings. Boys and girls drew Señor Cock and Señor Cricket. After several days, when the drawings were finished, the child read the book again, this time showing on the overhead projector the drawings the children had made on transparencies. Then the text's original illustrations were shown for comparison.

Table displays are popular devices used to share books. Simple backgrounds can be made, and three-dimensional objects can be placed in front of them to highlight scenes from books.

Mobiles can be designed by individuals or groups. Cutouts or realia tied to strings and suspended from wire hangers can make very successful literary displays.

Creative dramatics can also be employed. Children can make costumes of book characters and enact brief scenes from books. In one third-grade class this led to a Storybook Parade. Each child chose a personal favorite character and created a costume; the group presented the Parade to other classes. Each child told who he, she, or it was (there are some strange characters in the land of children's literature), and told a bit about the featured book.

In another school fourth graders did a program entitled Faces From Fiction in which they made masks of favorite characters.

Younger children can have a great time using Maurice Sendak's *Where the Wild Things Are* (Harper, 1963) to create paper-bag monster masks. Just watch what they will come up with!

Children's books, imagination, and simple materials can be combined to offer all children exciting, worthwhile experiences, giving them their own tickets to venture on incredible journeys to the land of books.

PART THREE

"Happiness Falling From the Sky!"
Poetry

AFTER ENGLISH CLASS
Jean Little

I used to like "Stopping by Woods on a Snowy Evening."
I liked the coming darkness,
The jingle of harness bells, breaking—and adding to
  —the stillness,
The gentle drift of snow. . . .

But today, the teacher told us what everything stood for.
The woods, the horse, the miles to go, the sleep—
They all have "hidden meanings."

It's grown so complicated now that,
Next time I drive by,
I don't think I'll bother to stop.

Poetry!

There is nothing better in the field of literature to train ears and flash beautiful word-pictures before young minds. Where else can one find the imagery contained in poems? What other form of writing can say so much in just two or four or ten lines?

Poetry is like many dishes spread out on a smorgasbord table—you go around and select what *you* want. If you want to laugh, you can turn to the works of Ogden Nash, Edward Lear, or Shel Silverstein. If you want to go on an adventure, there are many to choose from. If you want poems about pigeons, pincushions, computers, chocolate, beavers, bears, fathers, fireflies, mothers, or moths—you can find them.

In the Introduction to his anthology *A Way of Knowing* (Harper, 1959), Gerald D. McDonald states:

> Poetry can be wittier and funnier than any kind of writing; it can tell us about the world through words we can't forget; it can be tough or it can be tender, it can be fat or lean; it can preach a short sermon or give us a long thought (the shorter the poem, sometimes, the longer the thought). And it does all this through the music of words.

The music of words! Such music should be spread throughout each and every day of a child's life, and it should appear naturally, unforced.

Long before children enter elementary school, they have heard sounds and rhythms of words. Radio and television advertising, with its jingles and catchy phrases, have filled their ears. Music has made them aware of rhythm, and before they can utter their first words, they will listen to a beat, sway, turn round and round, tap feet, or clap hands.

Fortunate children have been exposed to Mother Goose nursery rhymes and jingles; they will have heard them sung or recited, prior to entering kindergarten. In the busy lives of today's families, this luxury is sometimes impossible. Time just isn't spent this way—there is too much to do to keep a house running smoothly, to make a living, to provide the basic elements of life. Therefore, it is both the responsibility and the privilege of teachers to introduce Mother Goose rhymes and nonsense jingles to children, for this literature is an introduction to poetry as well as an important part of our literary heritage.

There are many reasons why Mother Goose has lasted through time. The rhymes are filled with action: "Tom, Tom, the piper's son,/Stole a pig and away he run." They have characters who become familiar quickly through ludicrous situations such as an old woman living in a shoe or a cow that jumps over the moon. They have repetition of words with alliteration, which young children love to listen to and say: "Hickory, dickory, dock . . ." "Little Tommy Tittlemouse . . ." "Wee Willie Winkie . . ." They are succinct and they are easily remembered: "Jack be nimble, Jack be quick,/Jack jump over the candlestick." They pave the road to simple poetry and to beautiful prose.

Mother Goose is a natural for children, and teachers should make sure they do not miss the lifelong pleasures that only she can give. Soon after Mother Goose, we should introduce poems by those master poets whose work is timeless: Christina G. Rossetti, A. A. Milne, and Dorothy Aldis. Later we should acquaint them with more contemporary poets such as Robert Frost, Carl Sandburg, Langston Hughes, Gwendolyn Brooks, Nikki Giovanni, X. J. Kennedy, and N. M. Bodecker.

In 1977, the National Council of Teachers of English (NCTE) established the country's first award for poetry, the NCTE Award for Excellence in Poetry for Children—presented to a poet for his or her aggregate body of work. As of 1982, the award is given every three years. Below is a listing of the recipients, to date, and a sampling of their books to share with students, to further acquaint them with the words of some of the best poets who have written and are writing verse for boys and girls. Dates in brackets following each name note the year the poet received the award.

David McCord [1977]: *One at a Time: His Collected Poems for the Young*, illustrated by Henry B. Kane (Little, Brown, 1976), is a 494-page bonanza of McCord's work. A "Subject Index" appended is just right for steering readers to works about such topics as the circus, the Laundromat, or Little League baseball.

Aileen Fisher [1978]: *Out in the Dark and Daylight*, illustrated by Gail E. Owens (Harper, 1980), is organized around the four seasons, representing some of Fisher's best poems reflecting nature.

Karla Kuskin [1979]: *Dogs & Dragons, Trees & Dreams* (Harper, 1980) is a representative collection of Kuskin's poetry containing introductory notes on writing and appreciating poetry, illustrated with her black-and-white line drawings.

Myra Cohn Livingston [1980]: One of the most prolific writers of children's poetry in the United States; her *There Was a Place and Other Poems* (McElderry, 1988) is a must for use in today's classrooms. The volume emphasizes interpersonal relationships, describing such situations as family life, divorce, and remarriage.

Eve Merriam [1981]: For a fine sampling of this master writer of wordplay, look for *Chortles: New and Selected Wordplay Poems*, illustrated by Sheila Hamanaka (Morrow, 1989), containing such delights as "Cacophony," "Windshield Wipers," and "I'm Sorry Says the Machine," a humorous look at our contemporary electronic inventions.

John Ciardi [1982]: Published posthumously, *The Hopeful Trout and Other Limericks*, illustrated by Susan Meddaugh (Houghton, 1989), features such characters as the fast fiddler of Middletown and a silly old skinflint named Quince. This is a good volume to share with students before introducing lessons in limerick writing.

Lilian Moore [1985]: *Something New Begins: New and Selected Poems*, illustrated by Mary Jane Dunton (Atheneum, 1982), includes fifteen new poems as well as selections from the poet's six earlier collections, including *I Thought I Heard the City* and *I Feel the Same Way*.

Arnold Adoff [1988]: *Black is brown is tan*, illustrated by Emily Arnold McCully (Harper, 1973), liltingly relates a story of an interracial family. In *Chocolate Dreams*, illustrated by Ture MacCombie (Lothrop, 1989), Adoff pays tribute to his favorite flavor!

Valerie Worth [1991]: *All the Small Poems*, illustrated by Natalie Babbitt (Farrar, 1987), contains Worth's previously published books in this paperback treasury.

Students can look in the school or public library for other titles by these poets, to aid in creating a display. After they are familiar with the work, they can create their own Poetry Award highlighting the life and work of a poet of their choice.

There is a multitude of poetry volumes. Again the question arises: What poems should we use? The best verse to begin on deals with familiar experiences; but as soon as children's grasps will permit, they should encounter through poetry unfamiliar worlds other than their immediate environs. Naturally the city child does not have the same experiences as the suburban or rural child. The city child's exposure to animals, lakes, meadows, and pastures may be limited. The suburban or rural child may never have been on a subway, may never have seen a skyscraper or apartment house, or may not be able to comprehend city noises or the hustle and bustle of city life. Such experiences are provided, however, through various areas of the curriculum, and whenever possible, poetry should naturally relate to ongoing units in social studies, science, music, art, and mathematics.

With the tremendous variety of poetry available today, it is not difficult to tailor poems to the special needs and individual interests of children. This approach to poetry will contribute much more to the child's appreciation of verse. Too often the unit approach is used, whereby teachers introduce, dissect, analyze, and assign poems for forced memorization for one or several weeks in the school year and then never offer poetry again. Listening to or producing any type of creative expression cannot be satisfactory during a rigid and regimented time period. Trying to introduce poetry as a separate unit will only destroy any love a child has for verse.

The taste for poetry is soured by the dissection of words, phrases, and lines such as:

What does this poem mean?
What does this phrase refer to?
What does the poet really mean?

If a lengthy discussion about a poem is necessary, the selection is not right for either the class or the moment. Poems should be shared for their rhythm, their visual imagery, and for the emotional response children feel when they hear or read them. Poems should be presented simply. Many times a short statement such as: "I am going to read you a poem about pizza!" or "Hey! Maria brought us a poem about a moving van today!" is sufficient motivation.

The follow-up to a poem is also an important part of poetry programs. We should not ask children if they like the verse just read. If children have the desire to say something, they will say it. If they do not, let the poem end with its own final words.

Poetry programs throughout the grades should have a variety of rhymed and free verse. Beginning in the early grades, free verse can be introduced. In the upper grades narrative verse and ballads can be gradually introduced along with poetry that evokes emotion, stirs the imagination, and causes children to think as they never have before.

Teachers must take the time to read poetry to their classes every day. Children should *hear* poems, for poetry is created to *be* heard. If we read poetry regularly, it will not be unusual to hear children ask to have their favorite verses read over and over again.

Enriching Children's Experiences With Poetry

An appreciation for poetry can sometimes be developed by encouraging children to write poetry and look for poems in books, magazines, and newspapers. Children can aid in producing poetry anthologies or poetry files for classroom libraries. These collections can be bound into booklets, filed in shoeboxes within the classroom, or put into large brown manila envelopes and tacked under the chalkboard. Poems can be grouped and organized by a class committee. Specific headings might include: Months of the Year, Funny Poems, Seasonal Poems, Science Poems, or Poems of Mystery. Poem cycles can be developed on topics such as Streets, Brothers and Sisters, City Life, Houses, or Food.

Children who contribute poems to a class collection can record their names on them. Opportunities will frequently arise when such files will be useful. For instance, when a child is disruptive or in an unhappy frame of mind, the teacher might save the day by reading the poem that he or she contributed to the class— perhaps just for a boost of morale. One teacher in a Harlem classroom uses an old adage in verse form as a means of discipline. If a child is unruly, she merely comments in a dramatic tone:

> Let no one say, and say it to your shame,
> That all was quiet here—until you came!

A poem might also be read—perhaps one written by a class member, someone from a former class, or a child from another place.

There will be times when the interest in shared poetry will be so high that further activities might be planned. For example, children can effectively pantomime or dramatize poetry. One third-grade classroom in Virginia produced a Mother Goose Festival. The children represented such characters as Little Bo Peep, Wee Willie Winkie, and Mary, Mary Quite Contrary. They acted out the familiar situations in an assembly program for the kindergarteners and first and second graders. Simple props and scenery were constructed, costumes were made, and background music was found and used to enhance the production.

Another teacher, in Cleveland, planned a similar program entitled Nature and the Universe. Children became stars, planets, and comets, as they dramatized and recited both original verse and poems they had collected from outside sources throughout the school year.

Children on every grade level enjoy relating poetry to art experiences, and various art media can be employed to interpret poetry. Moods, feelings, scenes, or characters can be painted, drawn, or sculpted. Attractive displays can be made by featuring children's artwork along with selected poems.

Using realia can sometimes provide further motivation for children to enjoy a poem or a book of poems. A stuffed toy teddy bear might entice youngsters to delve into *Bear in Mind: Bear Poems*, selected by Bobbye S. Goldstein, illustrated by William Pène du Bois (Viking, 1989), or a toy model of a dinosaur to whet appetites for my own collection, *Dinosaurs*, illustrated by Murray Tinkelman (Harcourt, 1987).

Designing greeting cards can be another incentive to share poems. Children can select an appropriate poem and illustrate it. The cards can be used for classmates', parents', or friends' birthdays, as get-well messages, or to be sent on special holidays.

A New York City teacher persuaded upper-grade students to create Poetry Book Advertisements. Children read many volumes of poetry and then each selected one particular book to advertise with posters. Results were both exciting and creative while serving to get other class members to read the volumes they had chosen for their projects. One example, to advertise Robert Frost's *You Come Too: Favorite Poems for Young Readers* (Holt, 1959) is:

> When the homework's done
> Your chores completed
> And TV shows repeated
> Don't sit and be blue
> Read Robert Frost's *You Come Too*.

Writing Poetry

When poetry is read frequently to children, when children are exposed to and made aware of beautiful language, they can try writing verses of their own. Children can be made aware of the many diverse forms of poetry. When poetry is mentioned, a child almost immediately thinks of rhymed verse: "One, two, buckle my shoe . . ." "Hey diddle, diddle . . ." "Me-you-true-blue."

In writing poetry, rhyme is not the essence. This is not to say that this area of writing should be totally avoided. Some children find it comfortable to produce couplets, triplets, or quatrains. They enjoy listening to the singsong of word phrases and delight in writing it. One third grader created "Prize Fight" while viewing a professional boxing match on television:

PRIZE FIGHT

Give him a left and give him a right.
Don't you dare let him win that fight.
Go into him and then come out
Watch that right! Knock him out!

A fourth grader penned:

MY SEED

The seed is growing deep inside
It cannot hide, it cannot hide.
It shoves and pushes, it bangs and kicks
And one day the world will know me.

The limerick form is a favorite among older boys and girls. The humorous passages of Edward Lear can set an example of style and form. The limerick is written in five lines: the first, second, and fifth lines rhyme; the third and fourth lines usually rhyme but need not.

Here are two examples of limericks from the witty pen of Edward Lear:

There was an old man of Dunluse
Who went out to sea on a goose.
    When he'd gone out a mile,
    He observed with a smile,
"It's time to return to Dunluse."

****

There was an old man from the Rhine
Who was asked at what hour he'd dine.
    He replied, "At eleven,
    At three, five, and seven,
And perhaps at a quarter to nine."

Other examples of limericks can be found in John Ciardi's *The Hopeful Trout and Other Limericks*, illustrated by Susan Meddaugh (Houghton, 1989), and Arnold Lobel's *The Book of Pigericks: Pig Limericks* (Harper, 1983), and the collection *Lots of Limericks,* edited by Myra Cohn Livingston, illustrated by Rebecca Perry (McElderry, 1991), featuring over 200 selections.

Writing poetry can grow out of a lesson or discussion on the five senses or the use of similes. Discussions might be held on a one-to-one basis when a teacher feels that a child or a group of children is ready for enrichment.

Introducing unrhymed verse forms such as haiku, senryu, cinquain, and sijo has become very popular in middle-grade classes, for they produce rewarding results. Each of the forms can be used to write about a myriad of subjects, and they provide the encourage-

ment and satisfaction of completing an assignment—
something that is important for all children.

In introducing the various forms to children, it is
interesting to arouse their curiosity before describing
the formula. For example, I ask children to tell me what
they think "haiku" means. I ask: "Would you *eat* it?
Sleep on it? *Serve* it? *Save* it? What *would* you do with it?"
Then I ask: "What country do you think the word might
come from?" and I list the various responses on the
chalkboard. Cinquain is usually guessed as coming
from France or Spain since *cinq* is French for "five" and
cinco is "five" in Spanish. Children are quite surprised
to learn that the term was coined by an American
woman born in Brooklyn Heights, New York—Adelaide Crapsey.

I also try to have the children discover the form
by reading several examples. Next I place an example
on the chalkboard, reinforce their discoveries, and let
those who wish to create some of their own. When they
have completed their work, I have them volunteer to
read the finished product to the class. Finally, a display
is planned to show off the compositions.

Many children naturally take to these forms and use
them throughout the year in various classroom projects.

Haiku

The haiku is an ancient form of Japanese poetry. It is
written in three lines with a five-seven-five syllable

count, respectively. Since the Japanese language differs from English, the form is changed when the original Japanese haiku are translated. The purpose of the haiku is to present a single thought or observation particularly related to nature and indicating a season of the year.

Share with students *In a Spring Garden*, edited by Richard Lewis, illustrated by Ezra Jack Keats (Dial, 1965), a beautiful, lush volume of haiku reflecting nature and the changing seasons. Keats' use of collage might motivate children to illustrate their own work with this art technique. *Wind in the Long Grass: A collection of Haiku*, edited by William J. Higginson, illustrated with full-color watercolor paintings by Sandra Speidel, is another treasure to share. (Simon & Schuster, 1991).

After being exposed to the form an eight-year-old wrote:

> Fly high little bird.
> Let wind glide you through the air
> To your resting place.

An eleven-year-old created:

> The moon is alone
> With no one to talk to but
> The stars in the sky.

Senryu

Senryu was named for the Japanese poet who originated this verse form. Senryu has the same form as the haiku, but it differs in that the topic may deal with anything—it is not restricted to nature or seasons. The senryu form concentrates on a single idea or the image of a moment. The use of this form gives children the opportunity to express their ideas on any subject.

> The wham of the bat!
> The yelling of the large crowd!
> "Out!" calls the empire.
>
> Fourth grader

****

> Go home little girl—
> Your parents are calling you.
> Go home! And don't cry.
>
> Fifth grader

Cinquain

> Endless
> Dirt road, real long,
> Always lonely, quiet—
> Feeling of no one loving you;
> Lonely.

This was sent to me by Sister M. Jeremy, S.S.M., of Wildwood, Pennsylvania, who stated:

> I had the children write a cinquain. It is amazing how such a short piece can hold such thought and beauty. I like especially "Endless." This child wrote hers just when her older sister was getting married and moving to Texas. She expressed her loneliness extremely well.

One of the reasons many children respond to cinquains is that the sensitivity and delicacy of the form almost commands an immediate reaction. Cinquain was originated by Adelaide Crapsey (1878–1914). It was not until a year before her death that she wrote and perfected the cinquain. The form contains five lines, generally in iambic cadence, and has a two-four-six-eight-two syllable count, respectively.

Two examples of middle graders' creations are:

> These are
> Two happy times—
> Watching a baseball game,
> Seeing your baby brother walking
> Alone.

****

> One day
> A horse ran fast
> He ran so fast that wind,
> Sunlight, and all the blue of day
> Flew gone!

Sijo

Sijo is a verse form that dates back to fourteenth-century Korea. In English the sijo form is written in six lines, each line containing six to eight syllables. Sijo is more difficult for children than the previous forms and should not be introduced until a child can handle syllabication easily.

Many children find this verse form lovely to listen to and read. If preceded by lessons with the haiku and cinquain forms, sijo can prove to be a challenging writing experience for upper-elementary and older children. An experiment with a fifth-grade class in Harlem produced the following results:

BALLERINAS

Lovely ballerinas dancing
On their toes. They twirl round and round
Gracefully! Their heads in the air—
Lovely maidens floating on air—
Jump up swiftly and calmly
And twirl around all the night long.

****

SNOWFLAKES

Hooray for white things falling
Fluffy white flakes of joy
Happiness falling from the sky
The feeling makes you shake.
A white wonderland comes in view
Hooray! Hooray! for snow.

While working with a group of children in Hartford, Connecticut, two Spanish-speaking boys with a paucity of English vocabulary wrote:

We like to see how machines work
Me and my good friend José Rosa.
The old pieces are all black.

The dirt goes to our fingernails
And the oil goes to our pants.
We have to use big and small tools.

Although the verse forms described above require special line and syllable counts, no child should be forced to write within these limitations. The required forms should be suggested, not enforced. Our aim as teachers is to get children to express themselves in writing. They will write better and more freely if we allow them to overstep rigid boundaries.

Three volumes to offer children in the middle and upper grades are *Knock at a Star: A Child's Introduction to Poetry* by X. J. and Dorothy M. Kennedy (Little, Brown, 1982), *The Place My Words Are Looking For*, selected by Paul B. Janeczko (Bradbury, 1990), and *Poem-making: Ways to Begin Writing Poetry*, by Myra Cohn Livingston (Harper, 1991). *Knock at a Star* is a compact volume intended to stimulate further interest in reading and writing poetry. *The Place My Words Are Looking For* is an anthology of modern poems with a unique feature: Thirty-nine poets share their poetry as well as their thoughts, inspirations, anecdotes, and memories. Black-and-white photographs of the poets enhance the usefulness of this collection. *Poem-Making* introduces different kinds of poetry, emphasizing the mechanics of various forms.

For teachers, my professional book *Pass the Poetry, Please!* (Harper, revised edition, 1987), expands on the genre to bring children and poetry closer together. In addition to a potpourri of poetry ideas, part 2, "From Mother Goose to Dr. Seuss—and Beyond" offers biographical sketches and interviews with NCTE Excellence in Poetry for Children Award winners, as well as poets such as Gwendolyn Brooks, Nikki Giovanni, Jack Prelutsky, Shel Silverstein, and X. J. Kennedy.

Nancy Larrick's *Let's Do a Poem: Introducing Poetry to Children* (Delacorte, 1991) is a handbook full of lively ideas to stimulate poetry activities through listening, singing, chanting, dance, and dramatization.

Myra Cohn Livingston's *Climb Into the Bell Tower: Essays on Poetry* (Harper, 1990) brings together her insights into teaching and writing poetry for children. Part 2, "Poets of the Child's World," discusses eleven poets and their works.

PART FOUR

"Am I a Author Now?"
Experiences With Written Expression

from
PENCILS
Carl Sandburg

Pencils
telling where the wind comes from
open a story.

Pencils
telling where the wind goes
end a story.

These eager pencils
come to a stop
. . . only . . . when the stars high over
come to a stop.

Children's writing must stem directly from common events that occur in the classroom or from experiences that are a part of their personal lives. These experiences can be real or imaginary, but they must be the children's own. Most children are often much less interested in writing than they are in reading. Many times they feel they have nothing to say or nothing to write about. The classroom teacher must constantly utilize a variety of devices and techniques that can provide content for written expression. A local field trip, an area of the social studies, a science activity, viewing a film, and listening to a live or recorded program are common group experiences that can motivate writing.

Today children come to school with a great diversity of culture, customs, and mores. This can pose a problem for the classroom teacher; on the other hand, it provides a constant source of new ideas and raw material with which to experiment. For instance, one teacher whose class was fifty percent black and fifty percent Spanish used an effective bulletin-board display to alleviate resentment between the groups in her third-grade class. With the aid of an inexpensive Spanish/English dictionary, she titled a bulletin-board display

IN SPANISH, <u>FOOD</u> IS <u>COMIDAS</u>!

Two lists appeared on the bulletin board; one showed Spanish words, the other showed their English translations:

fruta	is	fruit
sopa	is	soup
carne	is	meat
café	is	coffee
leche	is	milk
manzana	is	apple

Both Spanish and black children gained better knowledge of one another's language, and soon simple statements and stories were created in English and Spanish on experience charts.

Experience charts are excellent devices for awakening children's interest in writing. The use of such charts is quite common in the primary grades; the value gained from recording children's experiences on chart paper or on the chalkboard are immeasurable. The greatest advantage of making experience charts is that it is a cooperative process. The child speaks to the teacher, the teacher writes down exactly what was dictated, and the child knows it is his or hers.

Emily Stegossi, a teacher in Philadelphia, Pennsylvania, uses this approach to discuss and record children's initial responses to the four seasons of the year. The chart is posted, added on to, and used as a reference point for a variety of children's writing experiences:

	SIGHT	SOUNDS	SMELLS
SPRING	blue skies robins	birds insects	honeysuckle roses

	SIGHT	SOUNDS	SMELLS
SUMMER	butterflies	crickets	summer rain
	green grass	brooks	salty sea air
FALL	colored leaves	crackling	burning leaves
	pumpkins	BOO!	apple cider
WINTER	snow	sleigh bells	pine trees
	icicles	winds	roasted chestnuts

This device should be used on every elementary grade level, particularly with children for whom English is a second language.

Written expression provides the child with the deep satisfaction of being able to communicate values, needs, and emotional outlets. A fifth-grade child wrote:

> I feel so bad today. My ma had to go to work and was afraid to leave me alone in the apartment. Last night police were all over the place looking for someone with a gun. I wasn't afraid though. I told my ma how I could take care of myself. She felt better and went to work.

A sixth grader expressed the following about his neighborhood:

> My block stinks! It has cans and cans and cans all over the place and garbage and rats and ugly people always asking for monee. If the city would only clean up the place maybe the people would clean themselves up and become human beens.

During the Christmas season a fifth-grade boy created this parody:

'Twas the night before Christmas
And all through the house
Everyone was stirring, even the mouse.
The stockings were hung by the incinerator
In hope that the heat would come sooner or later.

Children will create and reveal their inner thoughts only to a teacher who will accept them for what they are. When children write like this—when they create from their hearts—it is useless to take a red pencil from the desk drawer and correct spelling errors or misuse of grammar and punctuation. If teachers attempt this, they will not obtain creative responses the next time around; inner thoughts will be kept inside, shielded, and deep feelings will be turned into superficial sentences. The idea of assigning one title to an entire class, such as "What I Did on My Summer Vacation," or "My Best Experience," or "Fire Prevention Week and What It Means to Me," is outdated and horribly dull!

A fourth-grade teacher asked her class to write on the topic "Here Comes the Snow!" She felt this was an excellent topic for *all* the children in the class to write about since it was a cold, wintry day and the first snowfall of the year had just begun. She distributed paper, gave last-minute directions, and told the class: "Write creatively now. You have fifteen minutes!" Several minutes went by. Suddenly the teacher looked up and saw Yael shaking, crying uncontrollably. She took Yael out of the room to calm her.

"What is the matter, Yael?" she asked.

The reply was: "I can't write about that stuff. The world is coming to an end! I'm afraid."

Yael was a new arrival from Israel and had never seen snow before in the town in which she lived.

The remainder of the class compositions were not half as exciting as the fast-falling snow outside the window. In the same school—just doors down the hall—a second grader remarked to his teacher: "Ya know what it looks like? It looks like someone havin' a pillow fight."

Writing is often painful for children, and there are some who just cannot put their thoughts into writing. Writing is painful for many adults, too, including professional writers. I am often asked by students if I like to write. I always retort, "I like having *written!*"

Even some of our most popular literary figures will attest that writing is not easy; nor does it become easier with success. In an interview with Dr. Seuss, I asked him how he felt about the enormous success of *The Cat in the Hat* (Random, 1957), and if, after writing it, other books had come about more easily. He replied, "Each time I start a new book, that cat squints at me and says, 'Seuss, I bet you can't top me!'"

Exercises in brief writing experiences can sometimes pave the way for longer writing activities. If teachers begin with techniques that are within each child's grasp and allow for a sense of completion and accomplishment, children will progress to more mature forms of written expression.

The techniques that follow include several writing experiences that have been tried and tested—and have worked!

Quick-Accomplishment Ideas

Using the Alphabet

A lack of vocabulary is both a handicap and a problem for children who try to record their thoughts and feelings in writing. The use of the ABCs has proven to be very successful on every grade level. One teacher whose class was studying Africa assigned letters to individual children. They in turn researched books and encyclopedias to find words to match their respective letters. Words were then placed on oaktag charts and tacked around the room:

> A is for African animals
> B is for bronze figures
> C is for crops.

Another teacher used this same idea for a science unit on rocks and obtained such results as:

> A is for alibite
> B is for bituminous
> C is for calcite.

I have used this approach with children to do a Children's Literature ABC. One group came up with this beginning:

A is for Anansi
B is for Bartholomew, who wore 500 hats
C is for Clifford, the Big Red Dog.

Projects can include making booklets or combining other forms of writing on charts—for example, poetry forms, riddles, or similes.

ABC toughies, such as Q, X, and Z, sometimes pose problems: however, careful research on the part of the children might reveal some surprises. When a fifth-grade class prepared a project on the westward movement, one child was stumped on the letter Q for several days. He finally found "Q is for quince," which led to a very dramatic quince-and-cracker–tasting party. The letter X can always be the unknown, and Z gives everyone trouble. An anecdote that is fun to share with children is that even telephone companies have had trouble with Q and Z—they left them off the telephone dials and touch-tone pads! This usually sends youngsters home to check to see if their teachers are right—and they will find out that they are!

Steer children into such projects by having them look for ABC books in the library. Today one can find alphabet books to appeal to children of all ages. Alphabet books, once only used with the very young child, are now being introduced on every grade level to motivate new interests in language. In recent years such ABC books have appeared as *A B C E D A R: An Alphabet of Trees* by George Ella Lyon, illustrated by Tom Parker (Orchard Books, 1989), featuring twenty-six trees from

Aspen to Zebrawood; and *The Calypso Alphabet* by John Agard, illustrated by Jennifer Bent (Holt, 1989), from A for "Anancy. Spiderman of tricky-tricky fame," to Z, for "Zombie. A walking dead. No laughing matter."

Children can explore a bevy of alphabet books including those that have been selected as Caldecott or Caldecott Honor Book selections. The only alphabet book to date to receive the award was *Ashanti to Zulu: African Traditions*, by Margaret Musgrove, lavishly illustrated by Leo and Diane Dillon (Dial, 1976), a large-sized volume explaining some of the traditions and customs of African tribes.

Six other alphabet volumes have been named Caldecott Honor Books:

Baskin, Leo, Hosea, Tobias, and Lisa. *Hosie's Alphabet.* Viking, 1972.

From "A/The armadillo, belted and amazonian," to "Z/A ruminating zebu," this oversized volume is illustrated in glowing watercolors.

Eichenberg, Fritz. *Ape in a Cape: An Alphabet of Odd Animals.* Harcourt, 1952.

Simple couplets depict animals such as "A/Ape in a cape," "Q/Quail on a trail," and "V/Vulture with culture."

Feelings, Muriel. *Jambo Means Hello: Swahili Alphabet Book*, illustrated by Tom Feelings. Dial, 1974.

From "*A/arusi* is a wedding" through "*Z/zeze* is a stringed instrument," this volume will enrich an understanding of Swahili, a language spoken across more of Africa than any other. Pronunciation guides and brief descriptions of each item are given. An interesting tidbit is that there are *no* words for Q and X because these sounds do not appear in Swahili.

Lobel, Anita. *On Market Street*, illustrated by Arnold Lobel. Greenwillow, 1981.

Inspired by seventeenth-century French trade engravings, Lobel's luminous paintings depict the shopkeepers on Market Street and their various wares—from apples to zippers.

MacDonald, Suse. *Alphabatics*. Bradbury, 1986.

An imaginary romp through the alphabet is presented in this large-sized volume where each letter of the alphabet is transformed into various objects such as a quail, tree, or whale, and incorporated into twenty-six full-color illustrations.

Petersham, Maud and Miska. *An American ABC.* Macmillan, 1941.

A volume paying tribute to Americana, illustrated by masters of early lithography.

Similes

Similes are figures of speech that are direct comparisons using "like" or "as." Provide children with several phrases such as "As white as . . ." or "As green as . . .". Immediate responses will probably be "As white as snow" and "As green as grass"! Many teachers become discouraged when children come up with such "ordinary" responses, yet what better examples are there? After discussing word comparisons and word imagery, allow the children to select their own words and look for unusual and exciting phrases. Examples from fourth graders in Newark, New Jersey, included:

As white as the new paint on my kitchen wall.
As green as my father's eyes.
As fluffy as the featheriest feather.
As cold as death.

Similes abound in poetry. Encourage children to look through favorite volumes to find several which can be shared and discussed.

A good book to steer readers toward is *As: A Surfeit of Similes* by Norton Juster, illustrated by David Small (Morrow, 1989), wherein Juster, author of the popular *The Phantom Tollbooth* (Knopf, 1961), stirs up a storm of similes in verse.

Definitions via Charlie Brown

Charles M. Schulz's "Peanuts" characters—Charlie and Sally Brown, Lucy and Linus van Pelt, and Snoopy— have opened up ideas for creative writing activities for elementary school children. The book *Happiness Is a Warm Puppy* (Determined Productions, 1962) has been effectively used on all grade levels to motivate young writers. One third-grade class experimented with "Misery Is . . ." and came up with:

MISERY IS . . .

when there is a power failure and your ice cream is in the freezer.

when a school holiday comes on a Saturday.

when your favorite magazine is at the dentist's and you have no cavities.

Sixth graders from Seely Place School in the Edgemont School District in Scarsdale, New York, defined happiness and sadness:

HAPPINESS IS . . .

having a best friend.

having school a half day and going to the movies with a friend.

****

SADNESS IS . . .

when all your sisters get a letter in the mail and you don't.

when someone gets candy from a friend and you don't get anything but a peanut butter and jelly sandwich.

going to the cemetery at night.

This technique is short and spontaneous, and permits easy success for all children.

The Five Senses

There are many ways to emphasize the five senses in written expression in order to develop children's ability to keenly depict those things they see, hear, touch, taste, and smell. Mary O'Neill's *Hailstones and Halibut Bones: Adventures in Color*, illustrated by John Wallner (Doubleday, revised edition, 1989), tells of various colors and what they evoke in our senses. For example: "Brown is as comfortable/As love . . ."; "White is a pair of/Whispers talking. . . ."

Children can be encouraged to write about colors that are or are not included in O'Neill's book, and to describe their own feelings and images of color.

Greens by Arnold Adoff, illustrated by Betsey Lewin (Lothrop, 1988) contains twenty-six odes to the hue.

Aliki's *My Five Senses* (Harper, revised edition, 1989) gives a simple presentation of the five senses, demonstrating some ways we use them, illustrated with bright, full-color drawings.

SIGHT

Pictures and realia can be used to motivate writing experiences. Pictures cut from calendars, books, or magazines can be grouped around a theme or used for creating captions and titles or for writing descriptions. Illustrated material or realia placed on an opaque pro-

jector can produce dramatic results. A group of fifth
graders wrote the following captions after viewing a
picture of a young boy holding his report card in one
hand and his dog in the other:

I wish my dad could sign blindfolded!

Oh, if I could only switch report cards for a day, then
everything would be all right.

Look, kid, I have my problems, too.

Take two aspirins, that's what your mother does.

Rover, I've got problems!

A sixth-grade class collected a variety of pictures of
cats and created captions about them. A bulletin-board
display entitled Creative Kittens in a main corridor of
the school, generated howls of laughter from every
grade in the building.

The power of observation can be developed for exciting, creative writing results. A group or a class can sit
in front of a tree and look at it as they never looked
before! They can describe another classmate in detail,
or write about things in the school or community they
have lived with but perhaps never noticed before, such
as the colors of street signs, the type of plant life growing between the cracks in the sidewalks, or the variety
of building materials used in the construction of houses
and stores. No matter how depressed an area is, some-

thing of beauty can be found nearby if children are encouraged to look for it.

Books illustrated with photographs can help children to look at a host of subjects in new ways.

Totem Pole by Diane Hoylt - Goldsmith (Holiday House, 1990), illustrated with vibrant, full-color photographs by Lawrence Migdale, describes how a Tsimshian Indian carved a totem pole for the Klallam tribe and the subsequent ceremonial celebration.

Bruce McMillan, the creator of many books of high-quality photographs, shows a day at a beach in *One Sun: A Book of Terse Verse* (Holiday House, 1990), containing a series of two monosyllabic words that rhyme (Sand/hand; Tan/man; Wet/pet) illustrated with exciting full-color photographs; a book that can be used to inspire students' own terse verses.

Pigeons by Miriam Schlein, with black-and-white photographs by Margaret Miller (Harper, 1989), and *Looking at Ants* by Millicent Selsam, illustrated with black-and-white photographs by Dorothy Henshaw Patent (Holiday House, 1989), brings a close-up look at these creatures rarely seen before.

Children can find additional books illustrated with photography to display, look at, read, and enjoy. Refer to the Winter 1990 issue of *The Web*, in which the theme "Picture This" offers many creative possibilities for using books illustrated with photographs. Two informative features appear: "Developing the Art of Seeing Through Photography: An Interview with Missy Larson" tells how she uses picture taking with children; "Preparing for Tana Hoban's Visit to Olde Orchard" relates how one school set out to welcome the renowned photographer who has created a body of award-winning children's books, using photography in a wide variety of ways.

SOUND

Sounds can motivate interesting writing experiences. The word "onomatopoeia" was written on the chalkboard of a fourth-grade classroom and defined as a word that imitates the sound it describes. Children quickly responded with phases such as "honking horn," "buzzing bee," "crackling crunchy cereal," "rain's pitter-patter," and "the swish of a broom." Another fourth-grade class in a Harlem school composed the following poem after discussing noise:

NOISE

Noise, noise everywhere
What to do! It's always there.
Bang! Pow! Zoom! Crunch!
Buzz! Crack! Crack! Munch!

In the air, on the ground,
Noise, noise, all around.
Dogs barking, cars parking,
Planes flying, babies crying.

Sh . . . sh . . . time for sleep
Not a single little peep.

Oh no—through the door—
Comes a noisy, awful snore.

Tick-tock—stop the clock.
Stop the yelling on my block
Close the windows, shut them tight
Cotton in ear . . . nighty-night.

Sounds of the city's machines and people, sounds of the weather, sounds in nature—crickets chirping, birds peeping—can all lead to many new writing adventures. Experiment with:

Open the window and what do you hear?
What does night sound like?
Compare city sounds to country sounds.
What sound does the seashore make?
What sounds remind you of winter, summer, spring, fall?

Music can be used to inspire many activities. The sounds of various instruments, rhythmical beats, and a study of the way musical effects reflect various cultures and environments can be used in the classroom.

Children will enjoy making and using their own rhythm instruments. Have them try to compose their own music to talk and write about, too.

TOUCH

A Touch Box can contain a variety of items such as sandpaper, wood and cloth of different textures, paper clips, foam rubber, and plastics. Each child takes an item from the box and describes what it feels like. Responses can be recorded on a chart; poems and stories can be written from the vocabulary lists developed.

A similar device is to create with the youngsters a Touch Me bulletin board display, on which children can feel objects. Interesting fabrics—silk, corduroy, leather, velvet—can be placed on the display with room underneath each to record children's reactions about the objects felt.

A Nature Table containing items with various textures was set up in a New Jersey classroom. Children would go to the table, feel the items, then prepare charts with simple sentences and drawings. "A *coarse* rock," "a *silky* flower," "a *bumpy* twig," and "a *pimpled* gourd" are examples of second graders' responses to nature's textures.

A Touch Hunt can be planned for any grade level. Take the children for a walk around the school or neighborhood. Encourage them to use descriptive words, phrases, and similes to report on the feel of the things they find. For added fun ask them to create nonsense words describing various textures, for example, "croochy," "sissling," "soft-nice."

An old favorite tactile book, *Pat the Bunny* by Dorothy Kunhardt (Golden, 1962), can be shared to help children in primary grades to find ideas for similar types of books.

Taste and Smell

A lesson to evoke responses to taste and smell stimuli was prepared in a kindergarten class. A display consisting of smelling bottles and tasting jars was set up. The children were asked to use their senses to guess what was in the bottles and jars. For example, they had to distinguish between sugar and salt. Since they are both white, the children had to taste the contents to identify them.

For a similar experience, children can write their reactions to the smells and tastes of a variety of foods arranged on a table in open containers such as yogurt cartons. Try vanilla extract, honey, vinegar, dried milk, and the like.

In a fifth-grade room, candy canes were distributed to an entire class and the words TASTE and SMELL were printed on the chalkboard. As the children ate their candy canes, they called out words or phrases that described them. SIGHT, TOUCH, and SOUND were soon added to the list, which when finished read:

About the Candy Cane

TASTE	SMELL	SIGHT	TOUCH	SOUND
scrumptious	sweet	red	sticky	crunchy
pepperminty	chemical-y	like striped toothpaste	gooey	crispy
lousy	bad	like a drill	slippery	noisy

TASTE	SMELL	SIGHT	TOUCH	SOUND
watery	good	like a barber pole	rough	like chewing on ice
hot		good to suck on	smooth	crackling
spicy		like candy	flat	baby biting on a nipple
delicious			round	like the ground crumbling
like chewing nuts			hard	
like lipstick			lumpy	
like something foreign				

Popcorn, licorice, peanuts, or fresh vegetables can be the basis for similar lessons.

Children can learn how the sense of smell is connected to our sense of taste. Cut an apple and a potato into cubes. Have the children hold their noses as they sample each. Next have them taste the apple and the potato again without holding their noses. This simple experiment is easy to execute and dramatically helps children realize how the senses of taste and smell go together.

When-They-Are-Ready Techniques

A Different Type of Newspaper
Teachers usually shudder when the cry "Let's do a newspaper!" is uttered. Images of copy machines,

wasted paper, and various committees fussing and fighting race through the mind. One way to overcome these anxieties is to use a bulletin-board newspaper that can be changed daily, weekly, or monthly. The teacher and the class can use this newspaper to report current events or specific topics or simply to inspire creative writing.

The title and the various columns of the newspaper can be decided upon by the class. Topics could be:

Trips	Weather
Interesting Events	Fashion
Class News	Picture of the Week
Poetry Corner	Personality of the Week
Riddles	Lost and Found Column
Comics	Cook's Corner

Upper-grade classes might select an editorial staff to manage the newspaper. Lessons in analyzing daily papers can be integrated into the project to further students' knowledge of journalism.

In the lower grades, children can report news events orally. The teacher can write the news on the chalkboard or on experience charts:

The elevator stopped running. Donna
My ball fell in the sewer hole. Tony
My mother is going to have a baby. Danielle

Placing children's names after their comments helps build self-image. In one class a child commented, "I know why you put my name after what I said. It was my idea, and you really care about my ideas, don't ya!"

Children in lower grades who have the ability to write have been encouraged to become reporters by one teacher's photocopied newspaper guidelines. The form below was reproduced and distributed to a class interested in the life of early humans:

News writing develops accuracy and terseness in both form and style. It is one area of written expression that should be encouraged and experimented with throughout all the grades.

Keeping Diaries

Keeping diaries is another form of writing that can be both practical and creative. An imaginary diary account of a trip to Fairbanks, Alaska, was kept by a fifth-grade class in a New York City classroom. Several anecdotes from this diary included:

Monday, 11 AUG.
Our boat, the *North Star*, left yesterday. We were to sail at 9:00 P.M., but they couldn't get it loaded in time. They had to build a cabin on deck for three cows they were taking to an agricultural school en route. It was 11:00 P.M. before we left.

Tuesday, 12 AUG.
It is pretty rough this morning. They are getting extra ropes to put around the cabin to anchor it so the cows won't go overboard.

Sunday, 17 AUG.
Yesterday we stopped at Ketchikan. Miss H. got a ball of crochet cotton, which cost three times as much as we pay at home.
Ketchikan is the salmon-fishing center.
The climate here is mild in winter and cool in summer.
When we reach Juneau, we will be in the heart of the Alaskan panhandle.

Fictitious diary keeping such as this can be used in a study of a neighborhood or community, Central or South American countries, industrial areas of the

United States, or any of the continents.

Diaries also afford opportunities for factual reporting. Records can be kept of:

daily weather conditions such as temperature and cloud formations;

information relating to scientific accomplishments such as an experiment in growing seeds;

highlights of class experiences that occur throughout the year;

events that occur outside school life, such as family happenings, play activities, personal records of height and weight, or an account of the way leisure time is spent.

Diary writing, besides calling for brevity and accuracy, also provides an outlet for thoughts and emotions. Often the idea of a class diary is extended: Children begin to keep personal diaries or journals.

Letter Writing

There are many areas in the curriculum that offer opportunities for meaningful letter-writing experiences. Seize such opportunities and encourage children to write. It is not always necessary to have every class member involved in letter writing—sometimes one child may write a letter containing the ideas of all. With children whose vocabularies and skills are limited, teachers may act as scribes and encourage the children to illustrate their letters.

Several activities can be offered to children when they are preparing letters. They can proofread letters for spelling, punctuation, and grammar with another classmate; they can tell what sentences or words in their letters gave them the greatest pride; they can be encouraged to use one word in each letter that they never used before. The basic rules and forms of letter writing can be discussed with the entire class and reviewed from time to time when needed. When children are acquainted with the many kinds of letters that can be written, they will write them—and they will do it often!

"DEAR ABBY" LETTERS

One of America's most prolific letter writers is Abigail Van Buren, whose column "Dear Abby" is the most widely syndicated in the world. You might select several of the letters that have appeared in her columns and discuss them and the responses given.

One sixth-grade teacher in New York persuaded his children to write mock "Dear Abby" letters for a bulletin-board corner. Some children wrote to the fictitious "Abby"; others in the class answered the letters. Here are several examples:

Dear Abby:
I was playing jacks and my cat swallowed my ball. What shall I do?

Jill

Dear Jill:
Try bouncing your cat.

Dear Abby:
I love long hair but my mother hates it! Yesterday she took me to the beauty parlor and cut it all off. What should I do?

Hairless

Dear Hairless:
Buy a wig.

Dear Abby:
My kid brother is always bugging me. What do I do?

The Bugged One

Dear Bugged One:
Use insect spray.

This type of activity appeals to youngsters. What child can resist being witty or sympathetic, or giving advice? The idea can be easily converted to correlate with social studies programs or to enhance the study of literature. Students can pose such questions as:

Do you really think I should have taken that ride?

Paul Revere

How can I avoid that Prince running all over town looking for a girl with a glass slipper? Who does he think he is?

Cinderella

THANK-YOU LETTERS

Thank-you letters can be written to parents who helped the class in some way, the custodian who keeps the school clean, the police officer or crossing guard on the corner, or to a class member who contributed something special. In one school a class celebrated a Thank-You Letter Week during which notes were sent to everyone who did an extra something special for them. The class compiled a list of thirty-three persons to whom they wrote.

In another school a fifth grader wrote to the owner of a local pet shop thanking him for giving the class a gift of several white mice:

Dear Sir:
Thank you for the family of mice you gave to our class. I have been very fascinated with their actions and movements. I have studied white mice at home. I have studied the mice and find their reactions to be similar to the ones we have in class.
I have a question to ask. Would a mouse live longer if it was in its natural habitat or if it is kept in a cage as a pet? Again, I thank you for the mice.

PEN-PAL LETTERS

Students can have rich experiences corresponding with pen pals. Pen pals can be from nearby towns or cities or from a foreign country. In cities where the population is spread out—for example, San Juan or Los Angeles—children can correspond with intra-city pen pals. This increases the likelihood of the children meeting one day and offers an incentive for keeping an ongoing letter-writing relationship.

Judith DeToth's fourth graders at the Pequenakonck Elementary School in North Salem, an upstate New York community, began a pen-pal project writing to a class of students in P.S. 87, an inner-city Bronx school.

Toward the end of the year a trip was arranged for the Bronx pupils to visit their pen-pal friends in North Salem. Although none of the children had ever met before in person, the youngsters were quite familiar with one another upon meeting because of their exchange of letters and videocassettes.

The students of Claire Doran, a special-education fourth- and fifth-grade teacher at Oakside Elementary School in Peekskill, New York, began exchanging letters with a class of Navajo students at Tuba City Boarding School, an all-Navajo school run by the Bureau of Indian Affairs. After a time of exchanging letters, she planned a trip from New York to Arizona for a cross-country meeting of the pen pals.

In preparation, the students spent a year reading stories, viewing films, studying geography, and perusing pamphlets, gifts, and letters from the pen pals in Arizona. Her students, all from low-income families who had never traveled outside Peekskill's city limits, helped finance the trip by raising money, collecting

16,000 recyclable cans and bottles.

The young travelers met with a Navajo guide, drove to Montezuma's Castle, and traveled the Painted Desert, finally arriving at Tuba City. "I wanted my students to see there is something other than Peekskill out there," Doran said.

Although such projects might seem overwhelming, they can be done. And what an exciting learning experience this is for all involved.

GET-WELL LETTERS

Get-well cards, notes, or letters can be sent to classmates, teachers in the school, other school personnel, community figures, or convalescent adults. Everyone appreciates being thought of when absent from school or work with an illness.

LETTERS OF INVITATION

Letters inviting another class or perhaps a parent in to see a special classroom display or project can be composed.

REQUESTS FOR PERMISSION

A letter might be sent to parents requesting permission to go on a field trip or for permission to bring in something special from home. A child might write for permission to the principal to do something out of the ordinary, such as beginning a school club or team.

REQUESTS FOR INTERVIEWS

Interviews provide sound language-arts experiences for children. Students can write to community figures, school officials, or parents requesting interviews.

LETTERS TO FAMOUS PEOPLE

Letters to famous people such as government figures, scientists, artists, writers, or sports and entertainment personalities may be written throughout the school year.

On various occasions children have written to United States astronauts; television personalities in care of the stations that air their programs; and local, national, and international government figures.

Misha Arenstein, a veteran teacher in Scarsdale, New York, encourages his students each year to write Halloween letters and send them to famous personalities. One fifth grader in his class composed the following and sent it to Mayor Ed Koch, former mayor of New York City:

Dear Mayor Koch:
I am having a Halloween party and I would like you to come. It will be held at 666 Graveyard Road, Fang Island, New York. You can't miss my house. It is as big as five werewolves standing on top of each other. It is blueish-black. I live there with my daddy, my sister, and my Egyptian mummy.
Some of the other guests who will be coming are

Peter Graves, Boo Derek, and Red Skelton. For appetizers there will be fried bat feet or lizard tongues with blood sauce. Entrees will be grilled gorilla toes, munchy monkey tails, or sauteed salamander sausages. For dessert, we will serve chilled ghost pudding, crunchy crab cookies, and bat blood pie.

The Bloody River Slurp Singers will sing and the fifty-legged spiders will dance. Last year the entertainers forgot to come, so Murray the ghost did his disappearing act instead. If you are looking for me at the party, I will be dressed as Medusa. (Don't worry, my snakes don't bite.)

Sincerely,
Danielle

P.S. We will be serving Bloodweiser Beer all evening. Please write back.

Less than two weeks later, Danielle received a reply from Ed Koch, on official "Office of the Mayor" stationery, with the reply:

Dear Danielle:

Thank you for your wonderfully ghoulish invitation and the appetizing description of the monstrous menu.

While I would have enjoyed the scary festivities, I regret that my busy schedule kept me from attending your party. I appreciate your invitation and understanding. I hope you had a wonderfully frightening evening!

All the best.

Sincerely,
Edward I. Koch
Mayor

Children are always quite excited to receive replies from noted personalities. Letter writing of this nature contains built-in incentives.

For guidelines on writing letters of this nature, see Part Two, "Learning About Authors," page 000.

FRIENDLY LETTERS

Friendly letters can be written to pals, grandparents, newspaper carriers—or even pets! Children will naturally share many happenings through writing letters to friends.

NOVELTY LETTERS

Imaginations can run high when a novelty type of letter-writing experience is introduced. A third grader created:

Dear Columbus:
　　You forgot your unbrela.

　　　　　　　　　　　　　　　　　　Mother

Other examples include:

Dear Pencil:
　　　　　　Paper

Dear Needle:
　　　　　　Thread

Dear Pot:
　　　　　　Stove

Novelty letters can also be written after historical facts have been researched: Abraham Lincoln might "write" to Senator Stephen A. Douglas, Squanto to a pilgrim, or Harriet Tubman to a slave.

"Dear World" letters can come from students who pretend they are an endangered species, writing a letter to the world, pleading for their survival. After research and discussions are held, the children write their appeals. Below are two samples of fourth graders' work:

Dear World:
    I am the Bengal Tiger. I am a beautifully colored jungle cat. My only rival in strength is the lion. Sometimes I weigh as much as 500 pounds. My greatest fear is man!
    Man hunts me and kills me for my skin. Man has killed as many of my brothers as he can. We face extinction. Our life span is only about twenty years. We could survive if man left us alone. Please help us, World.

Dear World:
    My name is Pandy, the Polar Bear, and I'm mad. People are killing my friends by the hundreds. How horrible this is! Do you know why we are being killed? For our furs. They make coats and rugs from them. We can't even sleep because we're scared we'll be shot. Grown-ups don't listen. They just say, "Oh, well. That's a pity!" But it's not a pity if people just don't open up their ears and listen. That's why I'm depending on you. I know you'll listen.

REQUESTS FOR INFORMATION

A fifth-grade girl wrote to a government agency to ask:

Dear Sirs:

I have found from three different books that the color of George Washington's hair was red, auburn, and dark brown. Most pictures have him with gray hair. Can you tell me what color his hair *really* was?

A reply was sent:

The librarian at Mount Vernon tells me that, as a youth, George Washington had dark brown hair, verging on auburn. It started to turn gray during the Revolution and then became completely white.

Despite popular misconceptions, George Washington never wore a wig.

Teachers can provide children with the know-how needed to send for information when library materials are unavailable or do not include sufficient data to satisfy the extra-hungry young researcher.

Requesting information from embassies, chambers of commerce, industries, and organizations can also provide letter-writing experiences. Annette Frank Shapiro, a consultant for the Bank Street College of Education in New York City, uses a novel technique for securing information on the various states. She suggests that children find small towns or hamlets listed in an atlas and write to them. Smaller towns rarely receive such requests for information and are usually happy to accommodate children from other areas. In a Harlem fifth grade where this method was employed, children received letters from local mayors, photographs, newspapers, and town-event calendars. Such material makes a study of the United States take on new dimensions and provides for an exciting year's work.

Students might research such unusual or interesting place names in the United States as Kit Carson, Colorado; Panther Burn, Mississippi; Fly, Ohio; or Truth or Consequences, New Mexico.

LETTERS TO SHARE INFORMATION

Letters can be written to share information about new discoveries or new insights.

LETTERS OF OPINION OR PROTEST

Letters expressing children's opinions or protests might be written to focus on significant events. After carefully studying a particular issue such as pollution or the environment, discrimination, or drug use and abuse, students can write to local newspapers, governors, senators, or the president of the United States giving their views.

Children will be further encouraged when their pieces are printed in the "Letters to the Editor" column of their local newspaper or when they receive a reply from government officials. They then know that their words, thoughts, and ideas are listened to. Motivation runs high when students are involved in such meaningful letter-writing experiences.

Two books to share with children featuring letter-writing experiences are *The Jolly Postman and Other People's Letters* by Janet and Allan Ahlberg (Little, Brown, 1986), a "first-class delight" that children can open up to take out letters, each from its own envelope, and discover what well-known characters from fairy tales have written to each other; and Beverly Cleary's 1984 Newbery Award–winning book, *Dear Mr. Henshaw* (Morrow, 1983), containing a skillfully revealed plot through a series of letters written by Leigh Botts, a child of divorce, and Mr. Henshaw, an author.

Fables à la Aesop

Using Aesop's fables as models for writing can produce some impressive results. The fable is a brief moral tale conveying a wise saying or hint through the actions of an animal figure. One of the most popular fables by Aesop, "The Hare and the Tortoise," describing the famous race, ends with the admonition that "slow and steady wins the race."

Before children begin such a writing experience, acquaint them with a variety of fables by reading them aloud, or have the children read several selections.

A typical example from the lore of Aesop is:

THE CRAB AND THE FOX
A crab once left the seashore and went and settled in a meadow some way inland, which looked very nice and green and seemed likely to be a good place to

feed in. But a hungry Fox came along and spied the Crab and caught him. Just as he was going to be eaten up, the Crab said, "This is just what I deserve; for I had no business to leave my natural home by the sea and settle here as though I belonged to the land."

Be content with your lot.

Reputedly, Aesop, a slave, lived in the mid sixth century B.C. The first English collection of fables appeared in 1484. Although the fables of Aesop were not composed for children, they have always been popular with them.

In addition to Aesop, steer children toward contemporary books of fables:

Marcia Brown's 1962 Caldecott Award–winning book *Once a Mouse* (Scribner's, 1961) is a fable from India illustrated with striking woodcuts.

Arnold Lobel's 1981 Caldecott Award–winning *Fables* (Harper, 1980) includes twenty original tales (for example, "The Crocodile in the Bedroom," "The Ostrich in Love," and "Madame Rhinoceros and Her Dress") accompanied by the author's lush, full-color drawings and witty morals—"Even the taking of small risks will add excitement to life"; "Knowledge will not always take the place of simple observation."

A different approach is seen in two books by the folksinger Tom Paxton: *Aesop's Fables: Retold in Verse* (1988) and *Belling the Cat and Other Aesop's Fables* (1990; both Morrow), whimsically illustrated by Robert Rayevsky.

After a study of fables, Alex, a fifth grader in New York State, created:

THE LIONS AND THE LIONS

Long, long ago, in an African savannah, two prides of lions were roaming. Each pride had one male lion, and two female lions. In fact, the only thing that was different about the two prides was that one pride (who named themselves the Killers) had ten cubs and the other one (named the Murderers) had only four. The two lion families were enemies.

During nine months of the year, the savannah was filled with herds of animals. Thus, the prides could easily get food. The one problem was in the remaining three months (December through February), the lions couldn't find much food.

One day, during the three-month famine, a lioness from the Murderers spotted a young zebra and she quickly gave chase. Meanwhile another lioness (from the Killers) also saw the zebra and ran after it. They both pounced on the poor zebra, killing it. The Murderer proposed that they divide the beast in half, but the Killer wanted it all for herself. The Murderer did not agree so the two of them started a fight.

While the fools were fighting, a group of vultures swooped down and ate the zebra. The lions kept on fighting, and to this very day, on the very same savannah, those two foolish lions are still there, if not already dead, fighting over the zebra that isn't there.

Moral: Fighting does you no good.

Even Aesop would be proud of this piece of writing!

Biographical Data Service

Sixth graders in an Atlanta, Georgia, school originated this service for children in grades four and five. Teachers from the three grades met to plan the details before introducing the idea to the students. The plan was simple. Children in grades four and five were encouraged to write letters to the sixth-grade class asking them for additional information on famous personalities. The letters were brought to the sixth grade and read aloud by a student; interested children, either alone or in small groups, volunteered to do research on the personalities requested; when the work was completed, the child (or children) presented a lesson to the class that requested the information.

Various presentations were created, including a filmstrip showing, a panel discussion, the broadcast of highlights of a person's life over the school's public address system, the reading of part of a biography on the personality, and art projects in different media. Several children decided to cooperatively plan and write picture biographies for younger classes. These booklets became a part of the classroom library and were used throughout the school year. One group did the necessary research and writing, while others contributed their artistic talents to the production of the booklets.

A total of fifty such biographies, which included personalities from professions, occupations, the literary world, and the fields of sports and entertainment, were prepared during the year. This experience was beneficial for the children, for they were able to write in simple terms and yet receive recognition from teachers, peers, and younger schoolmates.

The Biographical Data Service has been successfully tried in school districts throughout the country. Several teachers have used this device to stir interest in contemporary black Americans. Children have written to Thurgood Marshall, former justice of the Supreme Court; entertainers such as Stevie Wonder, Diana Ross, Bill Cosby, and LeVar Burton; poets Nikki Giovanni and Gwendolyn Brooks; and Mayor David Dinkins of New York City to obtain information about their lives and their work.

The Service could be incorporated into ongoing classroom programs. Children could research past and current mathematicians, scientists, government leaders, or other groups of people in the social sciences.

Fourth graders at the Post Road School in White Plains, New York cooperated with eleventh graders at White Plains High School. Together the students wrote biographies of important women in their lives. The two groups met several times to study what goes into the making of a biography. Subjects of the biographies included mothers, grandmothers, and aunts, decided upon after the classes visited the International Center of Photography in New York City to view the exhibit "I Dream a World," featuring portraits by Brian Lanker of notable black women.

Upon completing the interviews, the students created their own books, which were displayed at the White Plains Public Library, where a ceremony was held to honor the young authors and the subjects of their biographies. Biographies focused in on the subjects' favorite childhood pets, sad family moments, and brave acts.

Patrice Williams, a fourth grader, relates: "When I wrote this book about my mom, I had the chance to listen to her tell me about her life, which she never tells me about."

This is an example of a writing experience that bridges age and grade gaps, bringing a project from within classroom walls out into the entire community.

There are scores of biographies that can serve as models for children's creativity. Introduce students to David A. Adler's "Picture Book Biography Series," which includes *A Picture Book of Martin Luther King, Jr.*, illustrated by Robert Casella (1989); *A Picture Book of Abraham Lincoln* (1989), . . . *Benjamin Franklin* (1990), . . . *Thomas Jefferson* (1990), and . . . *Helen Keller* (1990), each illustrated with full-color drawings by John and Alexandra Wallner (Holiday House). These easy-to-read volumes also provide brief time-lines of "Important Dates" in each of the subjects' lives.

Unusual Happenings

Sometimes an unusual, offbeat experience can be used to motivate children to write. The Chrysanthemum

Caper is one technique that can encourage young minds to run wild. One autumn Monday morning, I brought three huge, multicolored chrysanthemums into a fourth-grade classroom. The fresh flowers were put into a vase and placed on a table in the room. A lively fifteen-minute discussion about the chrysanthemums was held. The next day there was additional conversation about the flowers. The children continued to observe them and were asked to record their thoughts about the mums on index cards. This experience continued each day, becoming more and more stimulating. Naturally, toward the end of the week the flowers began to die; the petals fell all over the table and floor, the stems and leaves rotted and curled up, and the water became stagnant. The students in this class observed and creatively wrote humorous and serious stories and poems as they never had before. Their work was superior.

The Curious Cabbage was another technique used to rouse young interests. It is quite hard for children not to become curious at some point during the school day when a large, green head of cabbage is staring them in the face! The curious cabbage just sat on my desk until near the end of the school day, at which point I pulled a knife from my drawer and dramatically cored the cabbage. I presented each child with a leaf, as a gift, and told them they could do anything they wanted with it. Some children

threw it into the nearest litter container; others, however, played along. Carmen took hers to sleep with
her; Rodney studied his for several hours at home
and created a poem. The next day we talked about
the curious cabbage—how the children felt when
they first saw it on my desk, what they thought it
was for, and why I gave each one of them a leaf.

Many times the unusual or the unexpected is the very
thing that evokes wonderment, astonishment—things
that conjure new ideas—children's ideas—pure, inno-
cent, ever so beautiful.

Let's Make a Book

Creating books of their very own—taking a manuscript
from the idea stage through writing and illustrating and
finally to the finished, bound project, will reinvest
books with a unique value for students. Initiate a bookmaking project by first asking students to scrutinize
their favorite volumes. Encourage them to pay close
attention to every facet of a book, including dust jackets, bindings, endpapers, the title and dedication pages,
graphics, and indexes.

Set up a book-looking display table or shelf with a
rich and wide variety of books. Include the artwork
of Caldecott Award winners, as well as an assortment
of other illustrators' techniques: collage designs by
Leo Lionni; woodcuts by Fritz Eichenberg; photography by Tana Hoban; and a multitude of black-and-

white and full-color paintings by such artists as Bill Peet, John Steptoe, Susan Jeffers, Tomie de Paola, and Jerry Pinkney.

After a sufficient period of looking, suggest that the children begin making their own books. They will need to decide whether to work individually or team up with a coauthor and/or illustrator. Several students might wish to go outside the school, inviting older siblings, parents, and grandparents to lend a hand at illustrating their work.

Those eager to make their own books from scratch can consult *How to Make Your Own Books* by Harvey Weiss (Harper, 1974). The first section gives step-by-step instructions for making a book—including choosing paper, cutting and folding, binding and gluing to make covers, and deciding what kind of writing or printing to use. The second section presents a variety of book formats, such as comic books, diaries, scrolls, books of rubbings, and books of nonsense sayings. The volume is illustrated with photographs and drawings.

Part Two, "Making Your Own Books," in *Gifts of Writing: Creating Projects with Words and Art* by Susan and Stephen Judy (Scribner's, 1980) also provides numerous ideas on various types of books that students can create.

The Puzzle of Books by Michael Kehoe (Carolrhoda, 1982) follows bookmaking from writing and illustrating, editing, design, production, and binding until the volume is shipped to libraries or bookstores. The easy-to-read account is illustrated with numerous black-and-white photographs.

Aliki's *How a Book Is Made* (Harper, 1986) also describes the various technical processes leading to a printed and bound book, illustrated in full color.

In *If You Were a Writer* by Joan Lowery Nixon, illustrated in full color by Bruce Degen (Four Winds, 1988), a young girl, Melia, tells her writer-mother she would like to be a writer, too. As a day progresses, her mother gives her many helpful suggestions and helps her to see the joys of creating a story and to understand what being a writer really means.

Books: From Writer to Reader by Howard Greenfield (Crown, revised edition, 1989) gives older readers insight into the writing of a book and the inside workings of the publishing industry. This most comprehensive, lucid account of book production relates how a book is born, beginning with an author's idea through to the finished volume. Readers will truly enjoy this guided tour of publishing. Numerous photographs and drawings are included as well as a glossary, bibliography, and index.

Students will want to share their finished books. This desire can be satisfied in a variety of ways. Finished volumes can be given as family gifts for holidays or birthdays. They might also be donated to public or school library collections for others to read.

One school library media specialist in Maine includes

data on student-made books in the card catalog.

Third graders in North Carolina displayed their creations at a spring festival. Their teachers reported that a higher incentive for reading developed after students were involved in bookmaking projects.

Primary graders might design poetry shape books by cutting out basic shapes (squares, circles, triangles, rectangles) or the shape of a person or animal character from construction paper. The shape alone might dictate what the theme of an anthology will be. One first-grade class created an anthology called *Round Poems*, dealing with objects such as wheels, oranges, and other circular objects. After a batch of circles was cut out to form the book's inside pages, children wrote and illustrated definitions of a circle, opening with "A circle is round and round. It can never stop because no one knows where it started." Cutout circles made from colored oaktag were used for the book's covers. The children's copied-down poems made up the bulk of the anthologies. On the last page, they wrote a few lines "about the author," and attached snapshots of themselves.

Older girls and boys might write and illustrate stories for children in the lower grades. This is a particularly good project to launch with groups of children who are having difficulty with reading and writing skills.

Ideas such as these provide rich rewards for all students.

And So They Write

Writing sets a mood, an atmosphere. It helps develop imagination; it strengthens and adds to vocabulary development. It teaches that stories have plots with people and places running in and out and through them. Writing begins, goes somewhere, and ends! And the words set down on what was once blank paper become a part of time.

James tells of his adventure in:

THE MYSTERIOUS TOWER

I was walking along the country road one Halloween night. The clock struck twelve and then I saw an old broken-down tower. I went inside because the door was open.

When I got inside the tower, it was dark and gloomy. The door closed. I saw a head with the skin off. It was a skull without a body. Then a ghost came out.

The skull and the ghost were flying in the air. They began playing cards. The ghost played an ace. The skull played a king. Then the skull said, "Draw a card." I wasn't petrified at all. In fact, I wasn't even scared. Then the ghost and the skull both went away.

I went out the door. I walked into town tricking and treating. When I got home, I fainted!

Diane makes a wish:

ALADDIN'S LAMP

If I could find Aladdin's Lamp, I would make a wish to be a nurse because I like to care for babies. But since

I'm only nine and in the fourth grade, my seed is still growing. So I guess I'll keep on reading, and studying until I reach the top.

Donald wittily pens:

> Dear Miss Solomin,
> I just went a-swallowing
> and purposely caught the following:
> a duck in a truck, geese in a feast,
> a swan in a pond, a hen in a pen,
> and a pony in macaroni.
>> Tomorrow I will
>> have a new operation
>> and thanks very much
>> for your cooperation.

Another Donald inquires:

> I can't write no story just yet but I wrote this far so someday I will write a story but not just yet, does this make me a author anyhow?

Thus, writing showed James that he could gain satisfaction by discovering that he could build suspense and cause people to laugh with his clever use of surprise; it paved the way for Diane to imagine, dream; it gave a way for one Donald to show humor; it allowed another Donald to have the right to say he can't, yet express the hope that maybe someday he will!

Writing is many things to many people. In essence, it is a giving up of inner thoughts and feelings by someone to someone. Children do this readily, for they are the ones whose ideas are always fresh and new—even though the same ideas seem old and tired to an adult. Many things they do in life is a first—and so they write about it. Help them along, for if you do, not only will they write, but they will *want* to write.

PART FIVE

The Spoken Word
Oral Language

SCHOOL TALK
Lee Bennett Hopkins

We talk
about
science—
black holes in space.

We talk
about
people—
the whole human race.

We talk about
sand castles, sea gulls,
the sea—

When
can we
talk about
my
being
me?

A day begins in the life a child:

"Good morning, Ma."
"Good morning, son. Sleep well?"
"Yeah. What's for breakfast?"
"Watcha want?"
"Anything. Cereal and milk."

A day continues:

"Wanna play stickball with me?"
"Yeah."
"Let's go to the school yard and play."
"Great. Let's go."

A day ends:

"Shouldn't you be in bed by now? Shut off the TV and get to bed."
"Okay. Good night, Dad."
"Good night, son."

The spoken word. It is used every day in a variety of situations. It is the basic tool of communication—the primary form of verbal language. Children learn to use speech early in infancy. They begin by babbling, gradually making intelligible sounds, uttering a word, a phrase, a sentence, until they communicate verbally.

As children grow and develop verbal skills, they can be taught that just as there are different behavioral patterns, there are different social situations. As adults we can cite countless numbers of language roles used in our own lives—we speak one way as a teacher in the classroom, another with teachers in the faculty room, and still another at professional meetings. At home we change our language style and adapt it to family living; we change it again at the baseball game, at a coffee klatch with neighbors, at the opening of a new art gallery, or at a Saturday-night social affair.

Children should be made aware of these differences. They should not be made to feel that there is only one way to communicate, for if they do, their frustrations will mount, making them totally confused, thwarted.

The school day provides opportunities for developing oral language activities. Children should be allowed to tell something each day, if they so choose. They should be encouraged to share their personal experiences.

A third grader came to school one morning desperately wanting to share an experience with his teacher and class. His teacher was taking a rare opportunity to speak to a colleague about the adoption of a new reading series. The bell rang. The children were told to sit down and get ready for opening exercises. The flag was saluted, a patriotic song was sung, and then the class was instructed to "Take out your math books."

The child was uneasy, obviously disturbed. He wanted so badly to talk about something. A chance to speak did not come that morning. The rest of his school day was a waste for him. After school there was no one at home—no one to listen to his story about a dead cat he had seen in the gutter outside his apartment house, something that greatly bothered him. If this child had

had the opportunity to share this experience, perhaps the remainder of the day would have been more peaceful for him.

Asoli, a fourth-grade Japanese boy who lives in a posh upstate New York suburb, sees his mother for approximately twenty minutes in the morning before he goes to school. His mother, who holds an important position at the United Nations, and his father, a noted radiologist, both work in New York City. Asoli returns home from school at three o'clock, where a housekeeper takes over. He changes his clothes, watches television, does some homework, amuses himself with video games, eats dinner, and goes back to his room.

His parents return from the city at seven o'clock, sometimes later, spending an hour or two with him before he is sent off to bed. This is a lonely existence for any child—for anyone.

One of the few opportunities he has to converse—to speak—is in school. Asoli has been seeing a child psychologist for two years. His parents cannot understand his "peculiar" behavior when he fantasizes with an imaginary friend; his teacher cannot cope with his "disruptive" behavior when he talks out in class during the day. Is it any wonder *that* the child needs psychiatry? Wouldn't *you*? I would!

I always suggest that a few minutes each and every day be spent allowing children to freely converse with one another or to participate in a planned discussion with the entire class. Here views can be exchanged, ideas can be clarified, and an understanding of the amenities of discussion can be developed. Such an activity should not be considered a frill or a waste of time. We all know what it is like to want to share something. How many times do we rush to the telephone to tell our friends of exciting happenings in life:

I just discovered Philip's first tooth!
Nat got the promotion.
We became grandparents today!
Jenny was accepted at the college.

We cannot contain the excitement. We have to share—communicate—let others know that something has happened to us!

Children have more to share than we do, for they are always learning. We take for granted the surprise we felt when we first saw something new. The awe is no longer there when the curtain rises in a darkened theater, when we smell a freshly picked bunch of carnations, or when we look at the marvels of nature. As adults, we should keep in mind the wonder of childhood—the magic, the mystery, the miracles.

A few minutes devoted to a free flow of conversation will add greatly to the rest of the day, to the hours spent on teaching the basics, to the years of learning about life and its many complex components. Small talk can be big talk; it is an integral part of the curriculum—of life itself.

Using Recording Devices

Roberto, a fourth grader, was sitting next to the teacher's desk anxiously waiting for her to turn on the tape recorder. "Listen!" said Mrs. Alloca. "We are going to hear Roberto read a poem he read at the beginning of the year, and then hear the way he read it yesterday."

The recorder was turned on. Roberto and the rest of the class listened attentively. After a few seconds, Roberto remarked: "Is that me? Man, I don't believe it. Are you puttin' me on?"

Minutes later the class heard the same Roberto reading the same poem. The class was amazed at the speaking skills acquired in five and a half school months, but they were not half as astonished as the beaming Roberto, a new arrival from Santa Clara, Cuba.

Both cassette recorders and VCRs are all-important tools in the development of oral language experiences in elementary classrooms. They are widely available today, and they are simple enough for even young children to manipulate themselves. The anecdote above shows one way in which a recording device can bring about an early awareness of how speaking skills can be improved. Creative expression in other areas of language arts can also be enhanced if children are allowed and encouraged to use recording devices. Original stories, poems, and songs can be put on tape and played back for the class to hear or view.

In one of my sixth-grade classes, the children often selected favorite poems to read and record on tape. One day Richard, a quiet, sullen child who rarely participated in such activities, brought in an African war song he had found in a book of poetry. He showed me the poem and requested that I read it to the class. I stopped everything! As soon as the children were ready, I read the poem.

"Read it again!" Richard shouted when I finished. I read it again. This time, however, he began to beat upon his desk with a ruler, a beat that perfectly matched the cadence of the poem.

"Let's tape it!" he exclaimed. "Read it again, Mr. Hopkins, while I beat it out. I want to do that instead of reading the poem, okay?" Little did I know that at that very moment I had created a young Frankenstein's monster. By the end of the year I had read approximately twenty poems to the beat, beat, beat of Richard's enthusiastic drumming!

Richard's idea led to many new, exciting experiences. We began to discuss how effective the drumming sounds were as a background for poetry. Soon other children were looking for sound effects and recordings to suit the moods of their poetry selections. Within a month we had enough material to plan and produce a Poetry and Music Festival.

Intra-school broadcasts taped in advance are usually more effective than those presented live. In most schools, built-in facilities provide for broadcasting from a public address system. Programs taped in advance can be enriched with sound effects and musical backgrounds. An interesting series of broadcasts entitled "This Was the Day" was presented by fourth graders in Newark, New Jersey. Historical events, birthdates of famous people, holidays, and current local, national, and international happenings were carefully researched. A script was written, put on tape, and broadcast to other classes during a time convenient to their teachers.

Enrichment programs and the methodology related to teaching English as a second language offer numerous uses for recorders. Many elementary schools that teach foreign languages have set up foreign tape exchanges with children in other countries in lieu of pen-pal programs. Hearing children's voices or seeing the children in different environments, from other countries or other parts of the United States, can be quite exciting to all children involved in such a program.

Recording devices make possible many stimulating projects and can enrich oral language activities in all classrooms.

Choral Speaking

Choral speaking is an activity that can contribute to the appreciation and enjoyment of poetry as well as provide a worthwhile learning experience on any grade level with any group of children.

The easiest form of choral speaking is the *refrain*, in which children merely repeat the refrain or a frequently repeated line of a longer poem. After hearing a selection several times, children quickly learn when the line will appear and reappear, and they will wait anxiously for their cue to participate. "The House That Jack Built" is a perfect selection to use with even the youngest child.

A second type of arrangement is *two-part speaking*. Two groups of children take a part of a poem. A good example is the nursery rhyme:

THE PIE

ALL: Who made the pie?
BOYS: I did.
ALL: Who stole the pie?
GIRLS: He did.
ALL: Who found the pie?
BOYS: She did.
GIRLS: Who ate the pie?
BOYS: You did.
GIRLS: Who cried for pie?
ALL: We all did!

Line-a-child arrangements are somewhat difficult, yet they give each child a chance to speak one or more lines alone. The difficulty arises from the necessity for precision of delivery.

In *part speaking*, varied groups of children take parts of the selection. The teacher has the responsibility of knowing which children can handle the various speaking assignments. Here is one example:

THE KEY OF THE KINGDOM

ALL:	This is the key of the kingdom:
GIRLS:	In that kingdom is a city,
BOYS:	In that city is a town,
SOLO:	In that town there is a street.
SOLO:	In that street there winds a lane,
ALL:	In that lane there is a yard,
BOYS:	In that yard there is a house,
GIRLS:	In that house there waits a room.
SOLO:	In that room there is a bed.
SOLO:	On that bed there is a basket,
ALL:	A basket of flowers.
SOLO:	Flowers in the basket,
SOLO:	Basket on the bed,
SOLO:	Bed in the chamber,
ALL:	Chamber in the house,
GIRLS:	House in the weedy yard,
BOYS:	Yard in the winding lane,
SOLO:	Lane in the broad street,
SOLO:	Street in the high town,
BOYS:	Town in the city,
GIRS:	City in the kingdom,
ALL:	This is the key of the kingdom.

The most difficult type of choral speech is *unison speaking*, for it involves all the children speaking at the same time. Perfect timing, balance, phrasing, inflection, and pronunciation are required. This takes much practice and is quite time-consuming.

Programs of choral speaking can be planned and enhanced with lighting effects and with interesting staging techniques, such as having the children stand in a semicircle, scattering them around the stage, or interspersing their readings with simple dance and mime.

The selection of material available in this area is vast. Look for suitable poems in anthologies of verse or for books of choral speaking in which arrangements have already been worked out.

An excellent teachers' resource is *Fun With Choral Speaking* by Rose Marie Anthony (Libraries Unlimited, 1990), which features Mother Goose rhymes and contemporary poetry, with ideas for implementing choral speaking in the classroom.

In *Let's Do a Poem: Introducing Poetry to Children* (Delacorte, 1991), Nancy Larrick offers a host of sound suggestions in chapter 2, "When Two or More Read Aloud."

Choral speaking helps develop good speech, provides the timid child with a degree of self-confidence, and gives many pleasurable moments of enrichment to language-arts classes.

Creative Dramatics

Thinking, daydreaming, imagining, playing, doing, and acting are all components of the art of being somewhere, something, or someone else. In the earliest years children's play is filled with acting. The block corner in the nursery or kindergarten is the place where youngsters instantly become grown-ups—putting out fires, constructing bridges, or becoming astronauts zooming into outer space. A doll corner is a place to imitate adult behavior—taking care of a new baby, diapering, feeding, nurturing it.

When children participate in dramatic play, they cooperate with one another, they begin to feel the need for exchanging ideas, they speak, they listen, their vocabularies improve, readiness for reading takes place, and pathways are opened to direct teaching phases of written communication.

In elementary grades, prop boxes can stimulate creative dramatic experiences. The entire class can build prop boxes with materials found around the school or home and with handmade items. Prop boxes can be built around such themes as a Plumber's Box, which might include various lengths, widths, and shapes of piping, simple tools, hoses, and nozzles, an old shirt and cap; an Astronaut's Box, which might contain a space helmet, spacesuit, boots, headphones, moon dust, and moon rocks.

Once prop boxes are introduced, children themselves will think of themes and begin to fill them. Visits to local junkyards, community shops, bakeries, the firehouse, and hardware stores will aid in gathering materials. Parents as well as older children can add to the boxes.

Dramatic play will run high when such props are

available, and children's use of language will increase by leaps and bounds. Pantomime and dramatic play can be sparked by a cowboy hat, a necktie, or a scarf. Science, social studies, or mathematics can stimulate instant improvisations:

How did the cave man walk?
How do you think Newton looked when he discovered the principle of gravity?
How does your mother look when she forgets her wallet and she is holding up a long line in the supermarket?

Dramatic play is a natural step to creative presentations.

"A Journey Through the Middle Ages" was planned by a sixth-grade class. Children were divided into groups, each to deal with a specific aspect of medieval and Renaissance life. Books were brought in from the library for the Renaissance Research Shelf. Students began to peruse the books, using them as a reference source to convert the classroom to a medieval setting. A castle with towers reminiscent of the days of the Crusades was erected; a monastery and its gardens were produced in miniature; mural panoramas depicting feudal estates adorned the walls; spring sunlight filtered into the room through several windows decorated in the fashion of stained glass, an afternoon's art lesson. An original script was written by the class to include noblemen and noblewomen, knights and ladies-in-waiting, monks and nuns, serfs and pages. For background music and sound effects, the original Broadway cast recording of the Lerner and Loewe musical *Camelot* was played. The class learned several songs from the score to sing during their classroom pageant. The production was presented to all the classes in the school who came at intervals to see, hear, and *feel* life in the Middle Ages.

Once a class has been taken through such an experience, it is quite easy to repeat it. Actually, it is like putting pieces of a jigsaw puzzle together. Each group works individually preparing a project. The children then share what they have learned with other class members. Rough spots can be ironed out before presenting the program. When all the groups have finished their projects, a narrative is written to pull the program together. A few theatrical tricks—sound effects, lighting, musical backgrounds—all add a final touch.

Stories from the world of children's literature can become magic wands that transform children into Cinderellas, ogres and ogresses, beauties and beasts. Plays can be produced by posing such questions as: What scene will we begin with? Where does the action take place? Who are the characters in the story? What are they like? How will they walk, talk, move, grimace, react to various situations presented in the story?

A class of fifth graders I worked with presented a tremendously successful production of William Shakespeare's *Macbeth*. The students read and rewrote the original script, keeping, wherever possible, the Elizabethan flavor of the Bard's work.

Witches and murderers, ghosts and spirits, fiendish apparitions, and cruel, evil people with bloodstains on their hands were built-in motivating devices to stir the most difficult child. The escapades of Batman suddenly became a trifle dull and were reduced to a mere television sitcom level, while Shakespeare became second to none!

In one scene the script read:

MACBETH: My strong ambition makes me feel that Duncan should be killed. But how can I go ahead with my plan? Lately, Duncan has been speaking well of me.

LADY MACBETH: You fool! Don't you want the high position of King? Are you going to live your life as a coward?

MACBETH: Suppose we fail?

LADY MACBETH: We shall not fail! When King Duncan is asleep I shall give wine to his guards. They will fall sound asleep, also, and the King will be left unguarded. We shall place the blame on them.

MACBETH: If Duncan is to be assassinated, it would be best to do it quickly. We shall mark the guard's faces with Duncan's blood. This will throw suspicion on them. Everyone will think that they killed the King.

LADY MACBETH: Of course, who will dare think it any other way? We, naturally, will show our grief upon his death.

MACBETH: I agree. Ah, but I must hide my face from what my false heart knows.

In the coordination of the production, many specialists were brought in and many disciplines were crossed.

In art, children designed props and stage sets, made costumes from varied types of materials, and created the design for the tickets and programs. Music teachers brought in and taught Elizabethan music. "The 1600 Cushion Dance" was played by a small band ensemble, and a group of fourth-grade youngsters played recorders to add incidental music to the play. Creative dance forms were rehearsed for the famous banquet scene. The proper use of dueling weapons was taught for authenticity by the physical education department. In various areas of the language arts, children learned researching skills, engaged in creative-writing experiences, and learned a great deal about speech and acting through the rehearsal and actual presentation of *their* finished product.

Two children's books for older readers provide excellent guidelines for play productions:

Putting on a Play: A Guide to Writing and Producing Neighborhood Drama by Susan and Stephen Judy (Scribner's, 1982) includes tips on acting, ideas for plays and how to write them, and a chapter on Reader's Theater. "A Glossary of Stage Terms" is appended.

Writing Your Own Play: Creating, Adapting, Improvising, by Carol Korty (Scribner's, 1986), is a practical handbook giving advice, from choosing a story to dramatize through to the creation of the final script. A glossary of terms and a selected bibliography are appended.

Experiences in creative dramatics should be an integral part of every child's training, for creative expression heightens sensitivity both to children's own life problems and to their personal relationships with others.

PART SIX

To Think Is to Think
Critical Thinking and the Language Arts

SCHOOL DAY
Charlotte Zolotow

I don't mean to look
but I can't help seeing
a bit of sky outside the schoolhouse window.

I don't mean to watch
but I can't help watching
the maple branch that brushes against the pane.

I don't mean to dream
but I can't help dreaming
that I could be wandering
under the sky,

        watching the leaves
        watching the trees
        as the wind goes by.

Administrators, teachers, parents, and others concerned with youth constantly utter such comments as:

Tom, you're not *thinking*!
Did you *think* about that, Carlos?
Come now, class, *think* this answer through!

I overheard the following conversation while I was traveling on a New York City subway train:

MOTHER: Don't play with the umbrella!
CHILD: Why?
MOTHER: Because you'll hurt someone with it.
CHILD: Okay. But when we get outside, can I blow the umbrella up?
MOTHER: You're not thinking! You don't *blow* the umbrella up, you *put* it up.
CHILD: Blow it up! 'Cause it goes POP!
MOTHER: No, you say, "Put it up."
CHILD: Why?
MOTHER: 'Cause that's what they say! Let's go!

"You're not thinking!"

But was this child thinking? He certainly was. He was thinking the same way Tom, Carlos, or the whole class was thinking. Perhaps the thinking process did not produce the correct answer or response wanted by the teacher or another adult, but these children were *thinking*.

In today's society, in which children are confronted with a knowledge explosion that is almost beyond

adults' comprehension, there is a definite need to reex-
amine thinking and the thinking process and to utilize
every opportunity there is to develop clear thinking
abilities in children.

Long before children enter school, they actively engage in thinking. They explore the world about them;
in cribs and playpens they begin to look around,
contemplate. They select favorite toys by comparing
and analyzing. They begin to think! As children continue to grow and mature, they perceive their world
through sensory experiences, continuing to search,
to struggle with ideas. They perceive what is going on
around them—at home, in school, in the community, in the world. They begin to be critical of the
ideas and attitudes of others. They start to analyze
problems, uncover many different types of
solutions, and see relationships in the proper perspective.

This exposure to the trial and error of experience in
living, seeing, doing, and trying leads to early concept
formation—the ability to synthesize past and present
experience and knowledge for use in future situations.
The child who comes in contact with parents, teachers,
and peers who permit open-minded thought is able to
develop as a divergent thinker. Encouragement, opportunity, and experience can provide the key to this process, in which a learner discovers that there are many
paths to a correct answer.

We well know that even nonverbal children think. Once allowed to use their imaginations, to *do* rather than solely *memorize*, children bring their arsenals of experience and intuition to bear and are able to solve problems without the aid of textbook formulae. The essential stimulants are adults who encourage, provide opportunities, and believe in each child's ability to succeed.

The ability to learn to think is dependent upon a large number of factors, including mental and chronological age, physical, emotional, and mental state, and the child's experience with the total environment.

To think effectively, however, children must be taught those skills necessary to develop their thinking abilities. For centuries human beings have taught other human beings the basic skills for everything. The carpenter's apprentice learned how to measure wood, how to maintain and sharpen tools, and what tool to use at the proper time. The blacksmith learned how to shoe a horse—how to shape the shoe to the hoof, and how long to fire the metal. An apprentice learned the basic skills necessary to a particular job—in essence, learning a formula.

In early periods of American education, teachers also taught the basic skills—the formulae. It was common to find in children's textbooks typical problems such as:

Three children each have two pieces of string. How many pieces of string do the children have in all?

A formula was needed to find the answer to this problem; this formula was taught and had to be learned—usually without question.

What do I have to find out?
What does this problem tell me?
What do I know from this problem?
What do I have to do to find out the answer?
What will the answer be?

This type of thinking—convergent thinking—taught for decades throughout our schools, rested upon a narrow, textbook approach to thinking in which children were forced to memorize masses of data, learning formulae and then attempting to apply them to relevant situations and problems. The emphasis was on the *what*, rather than the *why*. The carpenter, the blacksmith, and the student learned their lessons in this fashion, or they were failures.

We must continue to teach basic skills, but we must go further. We must guide students to understand the *how* and *why* of problems, enabling them to become divergent thinkers. We must encourage them to find their *own* formula—to think for themselves. Situations occur in everyone's life where decisions have to be made, where there is no one formula. For example:

Should I accept that new job?
Should I join the Glee Club or the Camera Club?
What color should we paint the room?
Do we really need a VCR?
What crayon should I use now?
What can I bring in for Show and Tell tomorrow?

There are factors, other than basic skills affecting the thinking process, that grow out of a child's experiences. These factors—emotions, needs, attitudes, and habits—were termed by David H. Russell in *Children's Thinking* (Ginn, 1956), as early as 1956, "the motives for thinking"; they are motives that help to "initiate and determine the direction of thinking." Suffice it to say that the thinking process cannot be divorced from these motives and that these motives must be brought to the child's attention. Utilize every opportunity to help learners recognize what skill is needed where—what they are doing and why—for children can become cognizant that a final decision is attained only when they realize that such motives can, and will, affect their decisions. We must train youngsters to think for themselves and to think with clarity and precision.

We must encourage free-ranging inquiry and exploration, for these are needed to develop a divergent thinker; this is the type of thinker we must produce. Combining thinking skills with language-arts experiences is an excellent way of measuring and developing thinking abilities. Through language arts, thinking abilities can be put into operational terms—listening, speaking, reading, and writing.

The thinking process includes five basic components: observing, classifying, comparing, analyzing, and problem-solving or critical thinking.

Observing

Look out the window. What do you see?
I see rain. It look like the clouds are crying to water the flowers.

The plants need watering.
How can you tell?

You notice, you perceive, you observe.

Countless ways and countless opportunities occur every day to teach children to observe. We can take advantage of such opportunities to develop the sense organs:

What do you see?
What do you hear?
What do you taste?
What do you feel?
How does that smell?

Teachers can combine these opportunities with experiments to teach a pattern to follow and to teach how important observation is in relation to the thinking process.

An experiment was tried and tested with a group of second graders to sharpen their process of observation. The class was motivated to observe the formation of molds by discussing a slightly moldy lemon. Question after question was posed, and soon each child had volunteered to bring something from home to observe for the next few days.

I'll bring in bacon.
I'll bring in cheese.
I'll try a carrot.

Foodstuffs and materials were brought into class to be experimented with and to be observed. Children were given a form to record their observations:

MY MOLD		
Date:	What I Saw Today:	Statement about mold or a picture of the mold.

The children had a continuous experience with their observations, had the opportunity to follow through with their own experiments, and were able to observe the many other experiments taking place in the classroom. Records were kept, information was gathered by the boys and girls, knowledge sharing took place, and the class learned how to solve a problem using the scientific method. They identified a problem, collected relevant information regarding their problem, organized the information, and evaluated and compared their experiences with others in the class.

Thinking was going on here; sensory images were being explored. The classroom climate was perfect for learning, powers of observation were increasing, and the children's ability to think critically developed.

What other experiences can be provided for observing? A trip through the school can be an enlightening experience for students. Take them for a walk down the halls one morning. When you return to the classroom, discuss the things the children saw, things they have passed by time after time, such as the floors, doors, and the type of material used in the building's construction. Talk about the things they looked at and saw and the things they looked at and did not see. Go back again. This time, however, perceptions will be more acute, more varied. The children will be amazed to discover all the things around them that they never observed.

A third-grade class went on a walking trip through the neighborhood to look for city, state, and federal government services. The children were amazed at how much they saw within a few blocks—car license plates, mailboxes, sanitation workers, sewers, traffic signs—and learned what agency controlled each. Such an experience sharpens observation skills, teaches children to analyze simple phenomena, and prepares them for later classroom exercises in thinking.

Other opportunities for walking trips might be to observe the construction of a new house or building, noting the various steps involved, the machinery at work, the many types of workers and resources needed to put up a building; to see a neighborhood's architectural changes; or to observe language and numbers and how they are used in the neighborhood—for example, street signs and what they stand for, the use of abbreviations, house numbers, ZIP codes on mailboxes.

Such trips can be taken in any neighborhood. It is interesting to see what children can discover from careful observation. Historic sites, homes of interesting community personalities, or places of local importance might be discovered.

In Arlington, Virginia, one teacher takes her first-grade class to look at the same tree six times during the year. The children spend fifteen silent minutes carefully examining the tree. When they return to the classroom, they discuss what they have seen. The teacher records many of their observations, saving them to compare with their next visit. The many projects that come out of this firsthand experience could be utilized on any grade level.

Another teacher asks his fourth-grade class to bring an everyday object to class—a pencil, a milk carton, a saucer, a brush. These objects become the basis of a lesson on observing the unique qualities of each item. The children are told to look at their objects more closely than they ever have before and to rediscover details they may have taken for granted and never noticed, such as size, geometric shape, color, texture, and how and why the design fits the purpose each object serves.

"During your next meal, notice the color and the shape of the food you are served," requests a sixth-grade teacher. This becomes the basis for a discussion concerning emotions and attitudes toward food. Questions are generated such as:

How would you like to eat square peas?
Do you think you would like pink mashed potatoes?
Would green bread be pleasing to you?

This project reveals how we rarely look at or think about common, everyday experiences. In following class discussions, the eating habits of other cultures were introduced, and the similarities and differences of food were analyzed. An entire unit on the culture and customs of various groups of people evolved from discussions of Chinese food, Spanish food, and other foods commonly eaten in various parts of the United States. Samples of the foods were brought into the class to encourage many language activities.

Thomas Carlyle, the English essayist and philosopher, remarked:

> Shakespeare says we are creatures that look before and after; the more surprising that we do not look round a little and see what is passing under our very eyes.

Many opportunities and many experiences must be provided so that gradually learners will be looking *and* seeing. Their percepts will create new awareness, and they will become more conscious of their thinking. Let's encourage our students to begin to look around a little and see what *is* passing under their very eyes.

Classifying

From the time children enter kindergarten through the rest of their lives, they need to know, understand, and practice the process of classifying.

In the kindergarten and first grades, there are many opportunities to classify objects—to put things in order for more efficient use:

> Put all the red crayons in the shoe box.
> Put the puzzles with all the parts on the windowsill. If there are puzzles with missing parts, put them on the top shelf.
> Put the scraps in the paper drawer.
> Place your shell collection on the science table.

Through the grades, teachers can offer numerous ways to practice this skill.

> Which animal does not belong in this group?
>
>   leopard   cat   tiger   elephant
>
> Why doesn't the number 32 belong to this set of numbers?
>
>   3   9   15   21   27   32
>
> If a first-grade child sat in our sixth-grade class, how would a visitor be able to tell that the child might not belong?
>
> Arrange these circles in various ways:

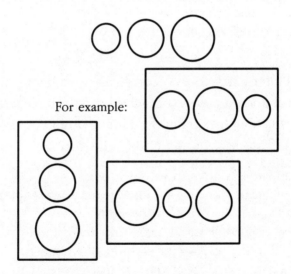

For example:

> All the above diagrams have a pattern or order.
>
> Are there other ways to *classify* them?

Classifying grows naturally out of the observation process; it increases a child's ability to recognize likenesses and differences; it teaches children to carefully observe items to be classified; it makes students more aware, more acute. Children must learn that there are many different ways to establish order. To do this, however, they must be provided numerous opportunities to collect, organize, and classify.

These experiences, tied in with other components of the thinking process, will lead to clearer thinking.

Comparing

José's taller than me.
I've got the same dress on as Marsha.
Your hair is straight, mine is curly.
My slice of pizza is bigger than yours.

Children are always comparing—noticing resemblances and differences. Teachers can promote, exploit, and utilize such experiences. Simple problems are surefire ways to set young minds in motion.

Compare this goldfish with that one.
Compare the ways we live today to the ways people might be living in the twenty-first century.
How do people travel across the desert in Egypt, compared to the way we travel through city streets.
Compare your answer with Donna's.
How are these two things alike? How are they different?

Working with children in any environment provides rich possibilities for making comparisons. Children are often lost and totally confused about a new environment. Children, however, no matter what area they come from, bring a rich heritage of culture and history. Many of the natural barriers of communication can be dispelled in school when children are given the opportunity to share and compare information about one another's backgrounds.

In many East Harlem, New York, schools, where the majority of the population is Hispanic, and in areas of Hartford, Connecticut, where there are many newly arrived Spanish-speaking children, my colleague Annette Frank Shapiro and I tried to capitalize on their backgrounds by developing contrasts and comparisons with the students.

Comparing, for example, the islands of Puerto Rico and Manhattan, we suggested the following activities to integrate various critical thinking skills with language arts and social studies enrichment:

START WITH GEOGRAPHIC ORIENTATION

• On a globe, a world map, and/or a map of the western hemisphere locate islands to survey topographical features; discuss routes of travel to and from New York City; stimulate critical thinking about the relationship of location, climate, and weather to food, clothing, shelter, and work habits.

• Take a boat or bus ride around Manhattan to compare island living. Note the rivers, the bay, the ocean, the shoreline, the natural harbor, and the links to other land bodies.

• Use putty or Plasticene in a large, flat pan, to simulate the geographic features of an island.

****

TRACE THE HISTORICAL BACKGROUND

• Compare the discovery and colonization of Puerto Rico and Manhattan.

• How do the traditions, customs, and languages reflect the influx of the diverse cultures that make up each island?

• What landmarks reflect the history of Puerto Rico? of New York?

• How has the political status of Puerto Rico changed since its earliest colonization? Why?

****

DEVELOP ACTIVITIES WITH CHILDREN

• Take a walk around the neighborhood to see evidences of Spanish culture. Observe language, food products, and plant life as a basis for discussion.

• Take a trip to a botanical garden to see flora and fauna indigenous to island living. Experiment in the classroom with plant growth by making a terrarium or planting bulbs, citrus fruit seeds, or potatoes. Record the growth on charts or keep daily logs of progress.

• Plan interviews using questions prepared by the entire class. Children can interview people from Puerto Rico. Parents, local merchants, and professionals may pave the way to further research.

• Make a large, three-dimensional economic, political, or historical table map showing Puerto Rico in relation to nearby islands.

• Broadcast the island's news over a classroom television station or over the school broadcasting system.

• If possible, establish a pen-pal or a tape-exchange program with a class in Puerto Rico.

• Make illustrated individual or class bilingual dictionaries.

Similar studies and comparisons can be made with any area.

Mass media provides excellent sources for making comparisons. After a discussion of a current topic appearing in a newspaper, suggest that students bring in the same story from as many other newspapers as they can. During the next few days, after comparing headlines and news reports, children will discover the many ways in which news stories can be slanted, how different writers and different newspapers interpret one incident, and, more important, the need to determine what is fact and what is propaganda.

Reviews in media can also be discussed. Reviews of books, television programs, sports events, and films can be analyzed and compared.

Comparing variants in children's books can lead to rousing discussions and activities. You might choose popular folk- or fairy tales, or nursery rhymes that have been treated differently by a variety of retellers and illustrators—for example, Lewis Carroll's *Alice's Adventures in Wonderland*, Margery Williams' *The Velveteen Rabbit*, Beatrix Potter's *The Tale of Peter Rabbit*, or the many ways Mother Goose verses have been interpreted.

Middle-grade readers will enjoy *A Telling of the Tales: Five Stories* by William J. Brooke, illustrated by Richard Egielski (Harper, 1990), featuring unusual retellings of five classic tales that raise new questions: What if Cinderella did not want to try on the glass slipper? What might happen if Paul Bunyan, the great tree chopper, met Johnny Appleseed, the tree grower?

A third-grade class was introduced to a study in which they were asked to peruse a variety of books on the Cinderella theme. Four volumes used in the study included: *The Egyptian Cinderella* by Shirley Climo, illustrated by Ruth Heller (Harper, 1989), a version of the story set in Egypt in the sixth century B.C., about a slave girl, Rhodopis, who eventually is chosen by the Pharaoh Amasis to be his queen; *Princess Furball* by Charlotte Huck, illustrated by Anita Lobel (Greenwillow, 1989), featuring a beautiful young princess who

runs away when her father arranges a marriage between her and an ogre; *Tattercoats*, collected and edited by Joseph Jacobs, illustrated by Margot Tomes
(Putnam, 1989), relating how a poor, neglected Tattercoats comes to marry the Prince; *Cinderella* retold by
Barbara Karlin and illustrated by James Marshall (Little,
Brown, 1989), an easy-to-read, humorous offering.

Children heard the different renderings read aloud,
read them on their own, and were asked about the
similarities and differences among the versions of this
age-old tale. They compared and contrasted the different styles of full-color art—how Cinderella herself was
interpreted by the various artists, from the regal queen
portrayed by Heller to the cartoon-style version by Marshall.

Plots, the costumes shown, and the relationship between Cinderella and the prince were analyzed and
compared. Finally, a group of children created their
own version of Cinderella.

This led to a similar study of "The Three Little Pigs"
in which four volumes were compared: *The Three Little
Pigs and the Fox* by William H. Hooks, illustrated by
S. D. Schindler (Macmillan, 1989), an Appalachian ver-
sion of the tale in which the pigs are named Rooter,
Oinky, and Hamlet; James Marshall's wacky rendition
(Dial, 1989); Margot Zemach's traditional retelling (Far-
rar, 1988); *The True Story of The Three Little Pigs! by A.
Wolf* by Jon Scieska, illustrated by Lane Smith (Viking,
1989), in which Alexander Wolf recounts his own out-

landish story of what really happened when he tangled with the three porkies.

Such projects can be done with any grade level, particularly with upper graders who are slower readers.

Comparing is one the most direct ways in which thinking takes place, and it is an integral component of the thinking process.

Analyzing

Examining propaganda in advertising offers excellent opportunities for children to develop the ability to analyze and to think critically. Today the mass media are some of the earliest propaganda influences young people encounter; they are constantly confronted with ideas expressed on radio and television. Hours are spent viewing shows that sell "the best cereal," manufacture "the biggest toy," or make you "the strongest when you eat our bread!"

Propaganda appeals to the entire gamut of our emotions. It does so without reference to clear and objective facts. Adults, as well as children, are tempted to jump to conclusions that are the easiest to come to. We *will* buy "the best cereal" if we hear about it enough; we *will* choose the largest package without stopping to find out how much *really* is inside the container. It is easier to do this than to stop and analyze the many parts of a problem and to arrive at one's own conclusions.

Children must be taught and reminded that pictures and words can have many varied meanings; they must be taught to examine, judge, be critical of words and pictures. Mental stop signs should appear when words such as *always*, *all*, *never*, *only*, *gigantic*, *fantastic*, or *stupendous* appear in speech or in print.

As early as 1938, the Institute for Propaganda Analysis identified seven basic techniques or types of advertising. They are:

1. Bad names—words with unpleasant connotations.
2. Glad names—words connected with pleasant feelings.
3. Transfer—when you buy a product you will transfer your feelings toward it. For example, brushing your teeth with Brand X will make you feel as glamorous or successful as the person who is using it in the advertisement.
4. Testimonial—well-known personalities endorse a product.
5. Plain folks—common, everyday people endorse a product.
6. Stacking the cards—telling only a part of the truth.
7. Bandwagon—everybody's doing it.

These seven patterns can be presented to children, to initiate a unit on analyzing advertising. Such a unit was tried with a fourth-grade group of students. They were asked to find out what kinds of soap were used in their homes and why their parents bought specific brands. The recorded session on the following day revealed:

TONY:　My mother buys _____ because it comes in a large bar and so many of us use it.

PEARL:　We get _____ because my mother says it helps our skin right.

SHARON:　Ours is _____. My mother buys it 'cause it's blue and it matches the bathroom.

DONALD:　We get _____ 'cause it's cheap!

IRVING:　My dad travels a lot and he brings home the little soaps from the hotels. We use that!

This session introduced a unit on analyzing advertising in print, on radio, and on television. Children collected advertisements and phrases from radio and television to match the seven basic types of advertising. Charts and booklets were prepared; original television advertisements were written and dramatized for analysis; local stores and supermarkets were visited; merchants and salespeople were interviewed to see if merchandise was purchased by consumers because of crash advertising or because of gimmicks such as sales, coupon come-ons, or giveaways.

Analyzing is an important skill for all children to learn. Children should be taught to recognize propaganda influences, for in all communities it is common to find sign after sign offering sales, discounts, and credit as a means to entice consumers and trap them into thinking that they are getting a bargain.

Ideas too must be analyzed:

- Do you think there will ever be an automobile manufactured that will run on electricity?
- Do you think a dog with long hair feels hotter than one with short hair? How do you arrive at your conclusions? Do you have facts or references to back up your initial opinion? How can you find out the facts?

These kinds of questions and activities are samples of exercises in analyzing, for general knowledge is needed to arrive at a conclusion. Hence, children will have to imagine, explore, research, and discover. Books will have to be consulted and read, experimentation will be done, and a new interest in the tools that one must use to analyze a problem will be awakened.

An analysis, after a thorough investigation, can be incorrect. It need not necessarily provide a solution to a problem. It is important for students to know and remember this. Analysis must be thorough. It must dissect each part, uncover every possible solution, weigh the meaning of each word, or detect every line in a drawing.

Children must be made aware that although they may recognize the many pitfalls, like those afforded by the use of propaganda devices, other motives may cause them to give in or "fall" anyway. A discussion of these motives—the emotions, the needs, the attitudes, the habits—will aid children in understanding and in evaluating the many ideas they encounter day by day throughout their entire lives.

When conclusions are finally reached, they will be the end result of a complete investigation. There will be an analysis, and repeated practice with this process will lead to clearer and more direct thinking.

Problem-Solving or Critical Thinking

One of the most important components of the thinking process is the ability to solve problems. Children, as well as adults, are besieged with problems throughout their lives. They range from the simplest type of decision-making such as: "What shall I buy with my allowance—a game or two packs of bubble gum?" to more significant problems that might affect one's entire way of life.

Problem-solving is a complex process that usually involves many other processes of thinking. In contrast to other areas of the thinking process, problem-solving depends more on precise, careful preparation and confirmation of the result.

There is no formula for problem-solving. People usually vary their own approaches to problem-solving from circumstance to circumstance, problem to problem. Two people presented with the same problem might offer different approaches and totally different solutions.

Certain general patterns of the problem-solving process, however, have been determined. These patterns are quite common in educational literature and are usually presented in six basic steps:

1. Identify and understand a problem.
2. Collect all relevant data and information related to the problem.
3. Select and organize data most relevant to the problem.
4. Formulate a hypothesis.
5. Seek all possible solutions.
6. Select the course that best solves the problem.

Although these steps are basic, not all of them would be used to solve every problem, nor would they always be used in the order given. Each problem must be met with an individual outlook and must be analyzed in a unique way.

Again, the "motives for thinking" enter into the solution of a problem; they may be helpful in finding the solution, or they may curtail the search for the solution. Much practice is needed in the complex process. It is important that the child be given many opportunities to discuss the *whys*, *hows*, and *ways* of problem-solving and be taught each of the steps in the problem-solving process. This takes a great deal of time, patience, and understanding, for these skills are not easily acquired. However, these lessons will be valuable ones; they must be taught, they must be learned, for they are important steps in thinking.

While these skills are being mastered, children will see themselves becoming more flexible in seeking solutions to the many problems they encounter. It is necessary to encourage children to try solving problems—not only problems in the mathematics textbook but real, living problems, the life experiences that all children have within easy grasp.

At the chalkboard, Ms. Levine was explaining a mathematics problem and was overjoyed to see a usually uninterested student giving his undivided attention.

"You're so interested, Charles, I'm sure you want to ask some questions."

"Naw, only one," drawled Charles. "Where do the figgers go when you rub 'em off that board!"

Charles posed a new problem—probably one much more interesting than the one Ms. Levine had presented. This could be the impetus for a whole new unit—perhaps a unit on problem-solving!

Thoughts on Thinking

Observing, classifying, comparing, analyzing, and problem-solving are all interrelated parts of the thinking process. For centuries philosophers have speculated about the workings of the human mind; the whats, whys, and hows of thought process are still being pondered by scientists and other thinkers today.

One of the most influential men in America to study the subject of thinking was John Dewey. His text *How We Think* (Heath), published in 1910, encouraged many more theorists in the field to explore the thinking process in works such as Jean Piaget's *The Language and Thoughts of the Child* (Harcourt, 1926); David Russell's *Children's Thinking*, cited above; Benjamin S. Bloom's *Taxonomy of Educational Objectives* (David McKay, 1956); Jerome S. Bruner's *The Process of Education* (Harvard, 1961); and John Holt's *How Children Learn* and *How Children Fail* (Putnam, 1965).

Many varied and different hypotheses have been expounded since 1910; some are excellent, some fair, and some will forever languish by the wayside.

One big question recurs time and time again throughout the literature: Can we teach children how to think? The answer is emphatically No! No one can teach another human being how to think. Our aim, as educators, should be to *help children to learn to think*—to learn the thinking process—not to teach them how to think. Such learning cannot be developed in connection with just one subject. It cannot, for exam-

ple, be related only to scientific experiments or mathe-
matical problems. It must be correlated with the entire
curriculum—with subject areas as well as personal relationships such as getting along with others, sharing,
and behaving in the classroom. It must be developed
continually and repetitively in the entire school curriculum.

We must focus our attention on aiding individual
children, to make use of the natural abilities they have
within them. We must teach the skills and mechanics of
the thinking process. We must cultivate the skills that
children use naturally and will continue to use in their
everyday lives. Then the learning situation will be more
realistic—and so will our goals. Then we can expect
results that are within reach. And when the child matures into an adolescent and the adolescent matures
into adulthood, we will have succeeded in producing a
thinking person.

We have a long way to go, but we can get there.

Perhaps one day when a child says "blow up the
umbrella" or "Where do the figgers go when you rub
'em off?" adults will not wince or scowl or quickly
respond with: "You're not thinking!"

Perhaps they will understand that these statements
are just as valid as, or even more valid than, when a
child responds: "Two plus two is four" or "Fourteen
ninety-two. It was fourteen ninety-two when Columbus came to America."

Perhaps they will learn to accept the multitude of

divergent ways of thinking that our fast-changing world will continue to require.

Perhaps they will begin to think much more about thinking.

Perhaps.

Afterword

In *Joys and Sorrows* (Simon & Schuster, 1970), Pablo Casals, one of the world's greatest musicians and humanitarians, reveals his passionate pursuit of beauty, justice, and compassion while living through an era racked by revolution and wars.

After reading the book, I reread it, noting a number of rich phrases, sentences, and paragraphs that leaped from the pages.

One such paragraph appears in the last chapter; it is a sentiment that I have always wished could be placed on walls, in halls, in every school in the United States of America—in every learning institution in the world.

Pablo Casals states:

> Each second we live is a new and unique moment of the universe, a moment that never was before and will never be again. And what do we teach our children in school? We teach them two and two make four, and that Paris is the capital of France. When will we also

teach them what they are? We should say to each of them: Do you know what you are? You are a marvel. You are unique. In all of the world there is no other child exactly like you. In the millions of years that have passed there has never been another child like you. And look at your body—what a wonder it is! your legs, your arms, your cunning fingers, the way you move! You may become a Shakespeare, a Michelangelo, a Beethoven. You have the capacity for anything. Yes, you are a marvel. And when you grow up, can you then harm another who is, like you, a marvel? You must cherish one another. You must work—we all must work to make this world worthy of its children.

We do work.

We try.

We try hard to "make this world worthy of our children."

We go on.

We strive.

We care.

We can.

We will.

We must—let them be themselves.

Appendix
Sources of Educational Materials Cited

American Library Association, 50 East Huron Street, Chicago, IL 60611

American School Publishers, POB 408, Hightstown, NJ 08520

Atheneum Publishers (see Macmillan)

Bradbury Press (see Macmillan)

Carolrhoda Books, 241 First Avenue North, Minneapolis, MN 55401

Children's Book Council, 350 Scotland Road, Orange, NJ 07050

Children's Literature Council of Pennsylvania, 101 Walnut Street, Harrisburg, PA 17101

Christopher-Gordon Publishers, Inc., 480 Washington Street, Norwood, MA 02062

Clarion Books, 215 Park Avenue South, New York, NY 10003

CRA Author Video Tapes, 300 Irvine Avenue, Suite 118, Newport Beach, CA 92660

Crown Publishers (see Random House)

Delacorte Press (see Doubleday)

Dell, Inc., POB 604, Holmes, PA 19043

Determined Productions, Inc., Box 2150, San Francisco, CA 94126

Dial, Inc. (see Viking)

Doubleday, Inc., 666 Fifth Avenue, New York, NY 10103

Dutton, Inc. (see Viking)

Farrar, Straus & Giroux, 19 Union Square West, New York, NY 10003

The Five Owls, 2004 Sheridan Avenue South, Minneapolis, MN 55405

Four Winds Press (see Macmillan)

Gale Research, Inc., 835 Penobscot Building, Detroit, MI 48226

Ginn & Company, 191 Spring Street, Lexington, MA 02173

Golden Books, 850 Third Avenue, New York, NY 10022

Greenwillow Books (see Morrow)

Harcourt Brace Jovanovich, 1250 Sixth Avenue, San Diego, CA 92101

HarperCollins Publishers, 10 East 53 Street, New York, NY 10022

Harvard University Press, 79 Garden Street, Cambridge, MA 02138

D. C. Heath Company, 125 Spring Street, Lexington, MA 02173

Holiday House, 425 Madison Avenue, New York, NY 10017

Henry Holt, Inc., 115 West 18 Street, New York, NY 10011

The Horn Book, Inc., 14 Beacon Street, Boston, MA 02108

Houghton Mifflin Co., 2 Park Street, Boston, MA 02108

Ishtar Films, Inc., POB 31, Patterson, NY 12563

Alfred A. Knopf, Inc. (see Random House)

Knowledge Unlimited, POB 52, Madison, WI 53701

Landmark Editions, Inc., 1420 Kansas Avenue, Kansas City, MO 64127

Libraries Unlimited, POB 3988, Inglewood, CO 80155

Little, Brown & Co., 34 Beacon Street, Boston, MA 02108

Lothrop, Lee & Shepard Books (see Morrow)

McElderry Books (see Macmillan)

Macmillan Publishing Company, 866 Third Avenue, New York, NY 10022

William Morrow & Company, 1350 Avenue of the Americas, New York, NY 10019

National Council of Teachers of English, 1111 Kenyon Road, Urbana, IL 61801

NCTE (see National Council of Teachers of English)

Orchard Books, 387 Park Avenue South, New York, NY 10016

Tim Podell Productions, Inc., POB 244, Scarborough, NY 10510

Philomel Books (see Putnam)

Putnam Publishing Group, 200 Madison Avenue, New York, NY 10016

Quackenbush Studios, 460 East 79 Street, New York, NY 10021

Random House, 201 East 50 Street, New York, NY 10022

RIF (Reading Is Fundamental), 600 Maryland Avenue S.W., Washington, DC 20560

Scholastic Inc., 730 Broadway, New York, NY 10003

School Library Journal, POB 1978, Marion, OH 43305-1978

Charles Scribner's Sons (see Macmillan)

Silver Burdett & Ginn, POB 2649, 4350 Equity Drive, Columbus, OH 43216

Simon & Schuster, Inc., 15 Columbus Circle, New York, NY 10023

University of Chicago Press, Journals Division, POB 37005, Chicago, IL 60637

Viking, Inc., 375 Hudson Street, New York, NY 10014

Frederick Warne & Co. (see Viking)

The Web, The University of Ohio, 29 West Woodruff Street, 200 Ramseyer Hall, Columbus, OH 43210

Albert Whitman, Inc., 5747 Howard Street, Niles, IL 60648

H. W. Wilson, Inc., 950 University Avenue, Bronx, NY 10452